"TELL HIM HIM HE'S PELE

...AND GET HIM BACK ON"

"TELL HIM HE'S PELE

...AND GET HIM BACK ON"

The Funniest Football Quotes Ever

Phil Shaw

EBURY
PRESS

1 3 5 7 9 10 8 6 4 2

Published in 2009 by Ebury Press, an imprint of Ebury Publishing
A Random House Group company

The Random House Group Limited Reg. No. 954009

Addresses for companies within the Random House Group can be found at
www.randomhouse.co.uk

A CIP catalogue record for this book is available from the British Library

The Random House Group Limited supports The Forest Stewardship Council (FSC),
the leading international forest certification organisation. All our titles that are
printed on Greenpeace approved FSC certified paper carry the FSC logo. Our paper
procurement policy can be found at www.rbooks.co.uk/environment

Mixed Sources
Product group from well-managed
forests and other controlled sources
www.fsc.org Cert no. TT-COC-2139
© 1996 Forest Stewardship Council

Designed and set by seagulls.net

Printed in the UK by CPI Mackays, Chatham, ME5 8TD

ISBN 9780091935979

Contents

1: 'Fleas in your pants': The players

When the captain said there was a problem at the back I thought he meant me and Steve Bould.
Tony Adams *after an Arsenal flight was delayed*

When Arsene first came to Arsenal, we called him Clouseau and then Windows because of those boffin's glasses.
Tony Adams

Dennis Bergkamp is such a nice man, such a tremendous gentleman, with such a lovely family. It's going to be hard for me to kick him.
Tony Adams *before facing his club colleague for England v Holland*

For me [being told AC Milan were interested] must be something special. It's like a boy being told Beyoncé is looking for them.
Emmanuel Adebayor

I no speak England very very well mate.
Anderson, *Brazilian midfield player, on MUTV*

The manager said I can have Monday off.
Darren Anderton *after scoring for Bournemouth in his last game before retiring*

Maybe if there was a bomb in the dressing room and four players broke their legs then I might get to play.
Leon Andreasen, *out-of-favour Fulham midfielder*

We needed Winston Churchill and we got Iain Duncan Smith.
Anonymous *England defender on Sven-Göran Eriksson's half-time talk against Brazil in the 2002 World Cup*

Q: What car do you drive?
A: Two Mercs and a Porsche.
Ade Akinbiyi *in a Crystal Palace programme interview*

I'd compare myself to Zinedine Zidane – a humble guy who just happened to be the best.

Nicolas Anelka

Italy turn up in Armani suits looking the dog's bollocks and we arrive in bright green blazers and dodgy brogues.

Phil Babb *on playing for the Republic of Ireland at the 1994 World Cup*

If we hide behind clichés we'll be dead and buried by January.

Darren Barr, *Falkirk midfielder*

England did nothing in the World Cup, so why are they bringing books out? 'We got beat in the quarter-finals, I played like shit, here's my book.' Who wants to read that? I don't.

Joey Barton

I'm one of the old guard. When I started playing you could kick owt that moved.

David Batty

At the end of Howard Wilkinson's team talks we'd be thinking, Eh?

David Batty *on life at Leeds*

When Charlie Cooke sells you a dummy, you have to pay to get back in the ground.

Jim Baxter

Ginola sold me three dummies and I was out of the game so long I had time for two hot dogs. To make it worse, he was polite to me after the game.

Darren Bazeley, *Wolves defender*

Of course I've been to Wembley before – for the greyhounds on my stag night.
Dave Beasant, *Wimbledon goalkeeper, before the FA Cup final*

What he said to us rang true, though his mouth sometimes loses contact with his brain.
Dave Beasant *on Dave Bassett*

Alan Ball and me didn't see eye to eye, and it had nothing to do with his being 5ft 3in and my being 6ft 4in.
Dave Beasant

Glenn Hoddle said I had no future at Southampton and agreed to sell me to Crystal Palace. Apart from that we got on great.
James Beattie

You can't compare me with Ruud van Nistelrooy. Maybe I could beat him at arm-wrestling.
James Beattie

At Real Madrid we all kiss each other before we go out. Playing for England against Jamaica, Aaron Lennon was going to replace me. I leaned forward to kiss him but then thought, Nah, better not.
David Beckham

INTERVIEWER: Would it be fair to describe you as volatile?
BECKHAM: Well, I can play on the right or in the centre and occasionally on the left.
Beckham *in an early TV interview*

There's no one to blame – they're just individual mistakes.
David Beckham

If I ever get round to doing a book, the title will be *Don't Google Me*.
Craig Bellamy *on his colourful past*

I've wanted to play in pink boots since I was little. The only way anyone can top me now is to play in diamond-encrusted boots.

Nicklas Bendtner, *Arsenal striker*

I understand nothing when Rio [Ferdinand] and Frank [Lampard] are talking. They speak Cocknik.
Eyal Berkovic *at West Ham*

Is there anything I'd like to change about my life? I took a penalty against Chelsea in 1971 and Peter Bonetti, the f***er, he saved it! I wish I'd sent it the other way.
George Best

Well, I suppose that's the knighthood f****d.
George Best *awaiting sentence in 1984 for assaulting a policeman*

Beckham can't kick with his left foot. He can't head a ball, can't tackle and doesn't score many goals. Apart from that, he's all right.
George Best

Is Rooney as good as me? Don't be silly!
George Best

When I was having my long goalless run [at Manchester United] people told me that if I'd shot John Lennon, he'd still be alive today.
Garry Birtles

Being at United was a culture shock for me. Even the loos had gold taps.
Garry Birtles

I was told they never used a ball in training at Barnsley, the theory being that we'd be hungrier for it if we didn't see it all week. I told the manager that come Saturday, I probably wouldn't recognise it.
Danny Blanchflower

It's our new tactic – we equalise before the others have scored.
Danny Blanchflower, *captain of Northern Ireland at the 1958 World Cup finals*

Blimey, the ground's a bit different to Watford. Where's the dog track?
Luther Blissett *at San Siro on joining AC Milan from Watford*

David Wheater comes in with these autograph books and asks players to sign. I say: 'Go away, I'm your colleague now.'

George Boateng, *Middlesbrough team-mate*

I must admit I have a dressing-room curiosity over Beckham. I want to see if he is equipped as he is in the underwear adverts.

Marco Borriello, *Milan striker*

John Byrne says his hair is natural. He must be using natural bleach.

Paul Bracewell, *Sunderland team-mate*

George Graham said just two words to me in six months at Leeds – you're fired.

Tomas Brolin

Gazza gave me three souvenirs – two fat lips and his shirt.

Steve Brown, *Wycombe Wanderers player, after defeat by Middlesbrough*

You score goals as a kid. Then you grow up stupid and become a goalkeeper.

Gianluigi Buffon, *Juventus and Italy keeper*

People say I'm eccentric because I go to bed with my goalkeeping gloves on, but I find people who blow £300 at the bookies eccentric.

John Burridge, *aged 46 and still playing for Blyth Spartans*

When you come to a place like Barcelona you think, Bloody hell, I wish I was back in England.
Terry Butcher, *Ipswich and England defender*

When the seagulls follow the trawler it's because they think sardines will be thrown into the sea.
Eric Cantona *to the media after escaping a jail sentence*

I'm glad there will now be two good-looking guys at Real Madrid. I've felt so lonely in such an ugly team.
Roberto Carlos *after David Beckham's arrival*

Mourinho is the funniest thing to come out of London since Del Boy and Rodney.

Jamie Carragher

You couldn't turn off the floodlights until Nobby [Stiles] had gone home because he needed to find his contact lenses after the game.
Sir Bobby Charlton

Someone said you could write Barry Fry's tactical knowledge on a stamp. You'd need to fold the stamp in half.
Steve Claridge

Me and Joe [Cole] went to a restaurant in Mayfair. The only other time I've been there was on a Monopoly board.

Peter Clarke, Southend player, on dining with his friend Cole before their FA Cup meeting

I never saw Razor hit Robbie in the airport, just the trail of blood going through the green Customs exit.

Stan Collymore on Ruddock v Fowler after a Liverpool trip abroad

INTERVIEWER: Which do you prefer, Rangers or Celtic?
ALFIE CONN: Spurs.

Alfie Conn interviewed on a TV documentary – Conn played for all three

Fergie showed me a picture of Uli Stielike before the final and I didn't think, World-class player. I thought, He looks like Basil Fawlty.

Neale Cooper, former Aberdeen midfielder, on their 1982 Cup-Winners' Cup final win over Real Madrid

Everyone was down the pub, drunk, the night before the FA Cup final. Probably what won us the Cup. That, and taking me off after an hour because I was delirious.

Alan Cork, ex-Wimbledon striker, recalls their shock victory over Liverpool

Matt [Busby] was the eternal optimist. In 1968 he still hoped that Glenn Miller was just missing.
Pat Crerand, *Manchester United player under Busby*

If I played for Scotland my grandma would be the proudest woman in the country, if she wasn't dead.
Mark Crossley, *English-born goalkeeper, on being touted for Scotland*

Paolo Maldini can say he has done it all now.

Peter Crouch *on AC Milan's visit to Fratton Park, Portsmouth*

I've played my last match, scored my last goal and elbowed my last opponent.
Martin Dahlin, *Sweden striker, announcing his retirement*

In the film *Kes*, Brian Glover thinks he's Bobby Charlton. Ron [Atkinson] is like that – he thinks he's the best five-a-side player at the club.
Liam Daish, *Coventry defender*

I got a text message from the FA saying I was in the England squad. It was too intellectual for a footballer to have written it. All the spellings and the punctuation were correct.
Curtis Davies, *Aston Villa defender*

What a player van Nistelrooy is. Even when he farts he seems to score.

Alessandro Del Piero, *Juventus and Italy striker*

I thought I had come to a chicken factory. It was also reminiscent of a Chinese women's volleyball team.

Ivo den Biemen, *Dutch striker, on life with Montrose*

The man who comes to take care of my piranhas tells me he will kill all my fish if I leave West Ham.

Paolo Di Canio

I want the West Ham fans to know that we're going to win something before I finish my career here. Otherwise I will kill myself.

Paolo Di Canio

How could anyone think the team would be better off without me?

Paolo Di Canio *after being dropped by West Ham*

When I kiss the West Ham badge people say, 'It's because he wants a new contract.' If I wanted a contract I'd come in here and lick the club's arse.

Paolo Di Canio *before joining Charlton*

For an away team to get a penalty at Old Trafford, Jaap Stam needs to take a machine gun and riddle you full of bullets.
Paolo Di Canio

Ray [Wilkins] is very strict on the dress code after being at clubs like AC Milan, where you have to wear a suit in bed.
Danny Dichio, *QPR striker*

Michael Owen has already given me a nickname. It happened quite naturally in training. It's Dioufy.
El Hadji Diouf *at Liverpool*

Wimbledon will take to Wembley. Once you've tried to get a decent bath at Hartlepool, you can handle anything.
Wally Downes, *ex-Wimbledon player, before the 1988 FA Cup final*

Before Molineux was rebuilt, there were cockroaches doing backstroke in the bath.
Keith Downing, *Wolves midfielder*

I like Quentin Tarantino films and stuff like that. There's nothing better than a good bit of violence.
Mark Draper, *Aston Villa midfielder*

I'd like to play for an Italian club, like Barcelona.

Mark Draper

Torres scored three but other than that I kept him pretty quiet.
Michael Duberry, *Reading defender*

My fondest memory of him [Mark Hughes] is his passport picture, which was a Panini sticker of himself.
Michael Duberry *on his former Chelsea team-mate*

I'm never one to make excuses, but I couldn't see the ball because the floodlights were in my eyes.
Damien Duff

Sam Allardyce knows what the club needs. He's done it at both ends.
Damien Duff *when Allardyce was appointed Newcastle manager*

I went into the Chelsea dressing room to swap shirts and it was bigger than my house.
Dickson Etuhu, *Norwich midfielder*

Before my Beşiktaş debut they sacrificed a lamb on the pitch and daubed its blood on my forehead for luck. They never did that at QPR.
Les Ferdinand

Danny Mills is the oldest 24-year-old I've ever met. He wears pyjamas, slippers, everything your grandad would wear.
Rio Ferdinand

Gary Neville was captain, and now Ryan Giggs has taken on the mantelpiece.

Rio Ferdinand

When he [Sir Alex Ferguson] starts with the hairdryer treatment on them, I've seen foreign players turn pink and black players turn white.

Rio Ferdinand

I don't drink except when we win a trophy. People must think I'm an alcoholic.

Ian Ferguson *after his 23rd medal with Rangers*

I don't make predictions. And I never will.

Paul Gascoigne

What's the world coming to when you get fined two weeks' wages for calling a grown man a wanker?

Paul Gascoigne

When Incey was running around with his head bandaged [against Italy], he looked like a pint of Guinness.

Paul Gascoigne

Coping with the language shouldn't be a problem. I can't even speak English yet.

Paul Gascoigne *joins Lazio*

I won't be doing the flute-playing bit I did in Glasgow. The gaffer has promised to buy me a guitar.

Paul Gascoigne *on joining Middlesbrough*

I didn't play many games for Middlesbrough towards the end of the season, or at the start or in the middle.

Paul Gascoigne

INTERVIEWER: When do you think you peaked?
GASCOIGNE: In two years' time.

Paul Gascoigne *on Soccer AM*

Q: Are you feeling your age? What do you feel like?
A: I feel like a kebab and onions.

Paul Gascoigne *interviewed*

Always seems to be about two stone overweight.

Paul Gascoigne *programme pen picture, Republic of Ireland v England*

[Ferenc] Puskas' left foot was so good he could even juggle the soap in the showers.

Francisco Gento, *Real Madrid colleague in the 1950s*

Claim to fame outside soccer: I once put together an MFI wardrobe in less than four days.

Terry Gibson, *Coventry striker*

If Dennis [Wise] fouls you he normally picks you up, but the ref doesn't see what he picks you up by.
Ryan Giggs

Kenny Dalglish was my boyhood hero. I even named my goldfish after him.
Ricky Gillies, *St Mirren player*

I may buy a yacht. It's the perfect way to pop back to France for a decent meal.
David Ginola *at the London Boat Show*

O! A diving lad.
David Ginola *anagram posted on the internet*

Roy Aitken told Mo Johnston to spit at Glenn Hysen's feet in the tunnel. Mo said he'd probably trap it and play it up the park.
Andy Goram, *Scotland goalkeeper, after playing Sweden in the World Cup*

Just because I play for England, [manager] Walter Winterbottom thinks I understand peripheral vision and positive running.
Jimmy Greaves *in 1960*

Playing for England won't faze Carlton [Cole] at all. One of his great attributes is that he doesn't think too much, so I think he'll be OK.
Robert Green, *West Ham and England team-mate*

My son doesn't think much of me. He's swapped stickers of me for Frank Lampard and Steven Gerrard. And he walks around in an Albion shirt with 'Robinson' on the back.
Jonathan Greening, *West Brom midfielder*

In the penalty shoot-out [Jerzy] Dudek looked like a starfish with jelly legs.
Bruce Grobbelaar, *former Liverpool keeper, after the 2005 Champions League final*

Scotland? They're a good team with strong English character.
Ruud Gullit *before playing for Holland v Scotland at Euro 92*

As a boy I was torn between two ambitions: to be a footballer or run away and join the circus. At Partick Thistle I got to do both.
Alan Hansen

Germany are under three times more pressure than us. I can see it getting to the point where they shit their pants.
Martin Harnik, *Austria striker, before the countries met in Euro 2008*

The Doc used to tell me: 'Be sure to get your late tackles in early.'
Ron 'Chopper' Harris *on Tommy Docherty*

You can never say never – unless you say never yourself.

Emile Heskey

I've stopped touching wood. I got splinters and was out for three games.
David Hirst, *injury-ravaged striker*

I'd only look as fast as Ryan Giggs if you stuck me in the 1958 FA Cup final.
Rick Holden, *Manchester City winger*

Q: Which sporting event would you pay most to watch?
A: Someone absolutely mashing Prince Naseem Hamed.
David Hopkin, *Scotland midfielder, in a newspaper questionnaire*

Michael Bridges' nickname is Germ. He always has a cold.
Darren Huckerby *on his then Leeds colleague*

Ally McCoist is like dogshit in the penalty area. You don't know he's there until the damage is done.
John Hughes, *Celtic defender*

First I went left, he did too. Then I went right, and he did too. Then I went left again, and he went to buy a hot dog.
Zlatan Ibrahimović *on a tight-marking defender*

I told Eric he couldn't go to court wearing a shirt unbuttoned to the chest. He said: 'I am Cantona. I can go as I want.' He got 14 days in prison and I thought, Oh my God, it must be the shirt.
Paul Ince

It's not nice going into Tesco and the till girl is thinking, 'Dodgy keeper'.

David James

Before the Man City game, Michael Owen texted me to say I'd better play well because I'm in his fantasy league team. After the game I texted back to say he'd better sell me.
David James after Portsmouth lost 6-0 to City and 4-0 to Chelsea

My mum actually taught me to knit. I knitted my teddy bear a jumper. I couldn't round off, though.
David James

Because I was small, Dad used to make me hang off the banisters for five minutes to stretch me. That was before I could have any dinner.
Lee Johnson, Bristol City midfielder, on his dad Gary, the manager

The Football Association have given me a pat on the back because I've taken violence off the terraces and on to the pitch.
Vinnie Jones

When I did a talk at Eton the boys were asking me things like: 'How big are Gazza's balls?'
Vinnie Jones

I'm still on the transfer list but Alex Ferguson has yet to take the hint.
Vinnie Jones

I can't run, pass, tackle or shoot, but I'm still here.
Vinnie Jones *on playing for Wimbledon and Wales*

My pot-bellied pigs don't squeal as much as Ruud Gullit.

Vinnie Jones

For some reason I thought I was signing for Howard Kendall – he was the only Howard I'd heard of.
Vinnie Jones *on signing for Howard Wilkinson at Leeds*

It wasn't that I was desperately late with my tackles, just a little slower in getting there.
Chris Kamara *on being a midfield hard man*

I have to watch Willy Wonka before every game. It's been my favourite film since I was a kid and gets me in the right mood for what lies ahead.
Malvin Kamara, *Huddersfield midfielder*

What do you have at Middlesbrough? Golden corner competitions?
Kevin Keegan, *then a Liverpool player, to an opponent during a negative performance by Boro*

At Hamburg you had to get to the dressing-room early to throw your towel on an empty peg.
Kevin Keegan

Personally, I like a hostile environment like the one we [the USA team] found in Costa Rica. Maybe it's because I played for Millwall.
Kasey Keller, *US goalkeeper*

I've known some greedy players – I remember wrestling with Gavin Peacock who's in Christians In Sport, for heaven's sake, when Newcastle had a penalty and I was on a hat-trick – but Bully takes the biscuit.
David Kelly *on Wolves strike partner Steve Bull*

The biggest difference between playing for Rangers and playing for Forfar? About £300 a week.

Stewart Kennedy, *a goalkeeper with both clubs*

I'm not the kind of guy who does the kind of thing I did. Nobody expected this from me, not even myself.
Kevin Kuranyi, *Germany striker, after walking out on the squad*

I thought there might be eight goals but I never expected we'd get four of them.

Dave Lancaster, Chesterfield striker, after a 4-4 draw at Liverpool

Stan Matthews used to put the ball on my centre parting. They don't do that any more.

Tommy Lawton

Q: Who do you room with and what's his most annoying habit?
A: Des Lyttle. He suffers from bad wind.

Jason Lee, Nottingham Forest striker, in newspaper questionnaire

Warren Barton's the best-dressed player I've ever seen. He even arrived for training in shirt, trousers, shoes, and his hair's lovely. We call him The Dog, as in the dog's bollocks.

Robert Lee

If I went upfield for a corner, I'd probably need a taxi to get back.

Jim Leighton on keeping goal at the age of 41

Colin [Hendry] isn't happy unless he's been kicked in the bollocks three times during training.

Graeme Le Saux, Blackburn team-mate

I'd have parachuted out of a snake's backside to leave Chelsea.

Graeme Le Saux at Blackburn, before returning to Stamford Bridge

[Gianfranco] Zola has always got the English–Italian phrasebook with him. Mind you, that's for him to stand on.
Graeme Le Saux

Throughout my career I've been described as 'cerebral', but I had to look it up in the dictionary.
Graeme Le Saux

The great thing about football captaincy is that when things go wrong, the manager gets the blame.
Gary Lineker *as England skipper*

I always score one against the Germans.

Gary Lineker *on being dismissed for one run batting for the MCC v Germany at Lord's*

Bobby [Robson] told me I could score lots of goals for England and put me on the bench for the first time against Wales. It brought me down to earth 20 minutes from time when he said, 'Get warmed up, Garth.'
Gary Lineker

There were plenty of fellas in the fifties who would kick your bollocks off. At the end they would shake your hand and help you look for them.
Nat Lofthouse, *Bolton and England centre-forward*

Germany are a very hard team to beat. They had 11 internationals out there today.

Steve Lomas, *Northern Ireland captain*

My most embarrassing moment was trying to follow Craig Burley's instructions in a Celtic game when he didn't have his teeth in, and getting it hopelessly wrong.
Malky Mackay

We had 51,000 to see us play Partizan Tirana and I think a lot of them came just to see what people from Albania looked like.
Murdo Macleod *of Celtic*

Sat in the stand, you're powerless to do anything. You've got fleas in your pants.
Florent Malouda *on being dropped by France*

For this whole being-alive thing, I can only thank the two beards, God and Fidel [Castro].
Diego Maradona *as a reformed drug addict*

We had an American player, Charlie DaSilva, who was on trial with us so long that the lads christened him OJ.
Chris Marsh, *Walsall midfielder*

SIR ALF RAMSEY: I'll be watching you for the first 45 minutes and if you don't work harder I'll pull you off at half-time.
MARSH: Blimey – at Manchester City all we get is an orange and a cup of tea.
Rodney Marsh, story of his England career

I did not know of Hull. I know nothing. Maybe with my satellite navigation I could find it. I would have no idea where it is on the map, though.
Obafemi Martins, Newcastle striker

After I joined Celtic someone in the street shouted 'Fenian bastard'. I had to look it up – Fenian, that is.
Mick McCarthy

I'd rather buy a Bob the Builder CD for my two-year-old than Roy Keane's book.

Jason McAteer, former Ireland team-mate

I was thrilled to be named fifth-best-looking sportsman in the world – until I learned Ivan Lendl had finished above me.
Ally McCoist

Kevin Keegan is the Julie Andrews of football.
Duncan McKenzie

It was wonderful to get on for my debut. Next time it would be really nice if I could touch the ball.
Gary McSheffrey, 16-year-old Coventry substitute

One manager sent me to Coventry for so long I thought I had signed for them.
Andy Millen, Hibernian defender

Three years at Port Vale is enough for anybody.

Lee Mills on leaving the Potteries club

TRAINER: How are you?
MIRANDINHA: I'm very well, thank you, how are you?
Mirandinha, Brazilian striker, on being injured while playing for Newcastle

Shunsuke [Nakamura] warned me that to become a great Celtic player I must not touch alcohol and chips. But I tried them one night and I won't be doing that again.
Koki Mizuno, Japanese Celtic player

My lasting memory of Roy Hodgson is that he always had a runny nose.

Dave Mogg, former Bristol City goalkeeper

I'd been ill and hadn't trained for a week. Plus I was out of the side for three weeks before that. So I wasn't sharp. I got cramp before half-time as well. But I'm not one to make excuses.
Clinton Morrison *after a mediocre display for Birmingham*

All I've got to do now is get the accent right.

Clinton Morrison *on becoming the latest Republic of Ireland 'Anglo'*

Big Ron remains a good friend and being called racist was a terrible representation of the man. Big Ron doesn't mean any harm to anyone. Well, apart from one time, when he hit Steve Orgrizovic in the face with a fish during a club trip.
Peter Ndlovu, *Zimbabwean striker*

I didn't understand why Gazza said he was taking his wallet on the pitch. Then he showed me a newspaper report where my mother said I would have been a footballer or a thief.
Marco Negri, *Rangers striker*

The only forward in the country whose first name is also an amphibian anagram.
Szilard Nemeth, *Middlesbrough striker, described in the West Brom programme pen pictures*

I've never been so certain about anything in my life. I want to be a coach. Or a manager. I'm not sure which.
Phil Neville

People reckoned I spent all my time in Stringfellows. That was nonsense. I preferred Tramp.
Charlie Nicholas

I was only a kid when Liverpool last won the league. In fact I was still an Everton fan.
Michael Owen *in 2002*

OWEN: I've worked my nuts off to get back from injury.
REPORTER: How are you feeling now?
OWEN: My groin's a bit sore.
Michael Owen *in a TV interview*

We named Sir Alex The Hairdryer because he would come right up to your face and scream at you.
Gary Pallister, *Manchester United defender*

I am a dreamer and this is one of my dreams.

Manuel Pascali *on moving from Parma... to Kilmarnock*

The atmosphere in the dressing room has changed completely. We feel more at ease. It is because Harry Redknapp is a very colourful person – we joke that he looks as if he comes to the stadium straight from the pub.
Roman Pavlyuchenko, *Tottenham striker*

I score more than 1,000 goals in my life, but the goal I don't score they remember.
Pelé *on Gordon Banks' famous save in 1970*

I was asked last week if I missed the Villa. I said, 'No. I live in one.'

David Platt *after moving to Italy with Bari from Aston Villa*

If we lived in another country we'd need political asylum. Since we're American we'll stay in New York and nobody will recognise us.
Tab Ramos, *USA midfielder, after losing 5-1 to Czechoslovakia in the 1990 World Cup*

Upon my little boy's head, I never said English players are overweight, knackered and drunk.
Fabrizio Ravanelli

Jimmy Greaves would walk past four defenders, send the goalie one way, roll the ball into the opposite corner and walk away as if to say: 'What am I here for?' then have a fag at half-time.
Harry Redknapp

I'm only 33 but my hair is 83.
Andy Ritchie, *Oldham striker*

One of the coaches at Brighton used to make us play five-a-side without a ball. I scored the best hat-trick you've ever seen.
Andy Ritchie

Of course I'm against Sunday soccer. It will spoil my Saturday nights.
John Ritchie, *Stoke centre-forward in the 60s and 70s*

I want a new squad number. The number 33 makes me look fat.
Gary Roberts, *Ipswich player*

The game's never over until the fat striker scores.

John Robertson *after scoring a late equaliser for Hearts*

They treat me like Maradona over here. I hope I can repay all this love on the field. I just can't score any goals by hand.
Robinho, *Manchester City's £32.5m Brazilian*

I thought, That's a sweet connection. I never even felt it touch my foot. Then I looked round and it's in the back of the net.
Paul Robinson, *England goalkeeper, on missing his kick to concede an own goal from a back pass against Croatia*

Gary Kelly is the maddest one at Leeds – without prompting, he was climbing head-first into wheelie bins.
Paul Robinson

Kanu is so laid back. Sometimes when he was playing I thought he was asleep.
Paul Robinson *on his former West Brom team-mate*

George [Cohen] has hit more photographers than Frank Sinatra.
Bobby Robson *on the England full-back's tendency to deliver wayward crosses*

Denis Law kicked me, right in front of the Queen, and I've still got the scar. It was worth it, though. England 9, Scotland 3.
Sir Bobby Robson *recalls the 1961 rout of Scotland*

Beckham's shirt smelled not of perspiration but of perfume. Maybe he sweats cologne.
Ronaldo *on swapping tops after a Brazil v England game*

I'm the first, second and third best player in the world.

Cristiano Ronaldo

I don't like to look like this [with a black eye], but in a few days I'll be beautiful again.
Cristiano Ronaldo

PRESENTER: You dropped your head when Pelé announced your name – was that relief?
RONALDO: No, I was just checking my flies.
Cristiano Ronaldo *at Portuguese TV's coverage of the Fifa Player of the Year award*

Berlin has everything. It's a cosmopolitan city with theatres, cinemas and open-minded people. Nottingham has hardly anything apart from Robin Hood, and he's dead.

Bryan Roy *on leaving Forest for Hertha Berlin*

We're 100 per cent behind Terry [Venables] – I've even taken down my Amstrad satellite dish and put it in the dustbin.

Neil Ruddock, *Tottenham defender, on the feud between Venables and Alan Sugar*

The biggest thrill of my life was being at my son's birth. I was there because I was suspended.

Neil Ruddock

Q: Which player is the worst trainer you have ever seen?
A: Mark Kennedy used to bring a cigar and deckchair into training.

Dave Savage, *Millwall player, in a* Sun *questionnaire*

Ryan Giggs is a fabulous role model. I've got a little boy and I want him to grow up like Ryan Giggs, not like his dad.

Robbie Savage

It's a great place to come to. When I saw the electronic gates and long driveway I thought I'd driven back to my own house by mistake.

Robbie Savage *at Derby's training centre*

My new yellow Ferrari broke down on the M42. I ended up on the side of the motorway with everyone driving past giving me the 'V' and 'wanker' signs, even old men and women.
Robbie Savage

I thought Swansea was in England, because they play there. But obviously I found out it's in Wales, which was quite shocking.
Jason Scotland, *Trinidadian Swansea City striker*

After the Nayim goal in Paris, people seeing me would totter backwards like I did, pretending to watch a ball sail over their heads.
David Seaman

We beat Newport County 13-0. And they were lucky to get nil.

Len Shackleton *recalls his six-goal Newcastle debut*

When you play for Scotland you look at your dark blue shirt and the wee lion looks up at you saying, 'Get out there after those English bastards.'
Bill Shankly

Paul Ince wants everyone to call him Guv'nor, but we call him Incey.
Lee Sharpe, *Manchester United colleague*

Cloughie called me Edward. I told him I preferred Teddy. He said, 'Right you are, Edward.'
Teddy Sheringham

Some of the young lads in the team would be bringing the house down if there was a house to bring down.
Neil Shipperley, *Wimbledon captain, after crowds fell to 2,500*

I don't understand Mr Ferguson when he is speaking normally, so when he yells it's even more difficult.
Mikaël Silvestre, *French defender with Manchester United*

I knew I was in trouble when I looked down and the leg was pointing one way while the ankle was facing towards Hong Kong.
Alan Smith *on breaking a leg with Manchester United at Liverpool*

I'm just as good as Peter Schmeichel, but I'm more modest by nature.

Thomas Sorensen, *Denmark goalkeeper*

The way Frank Worthington's losing his hair, he'll be the first bald guy to do impressions of Elvis Presley.
Graeme Souness

[Bobby Gould] would make a great double-glazing salesman. We had a meeting and by the end we were all thinking, When's he going to sell us a new car?
Neville Southall, *Wales goalkeeper*

I'm sure people will always say, 'He's the idiot who missed that penalty.'
Gareth Southgate *a year after Euro 96*

[John Gregory] handled the pressure brilliantly during our poor run, except when he smashed the physio's bag across Goodison Park.
Gareth Southgate *on his manager at Aston Villa*

Did he [Theo Walcott] have any weaknesses? Watching *EastEnders*.

Tim Sparv, *Finnish former youth-team colleague at Southampton*

A cold, damp dressing room is our secret weapon for Spurs, not forgetting their lukewarm pot of tea at half-time.
Phil Sproson, *Port Vale defender, before beating Tottenham in the FA Cup*

Franz Beckenbauer is like Humpty Dumpty and the team are playing like a bunch of cucumbers.
Ulli Stein, *West Germany's No. 3 goalkeeper, at the 1986 World Cup. He was sent home*

Peter Schmeichel reckons the present Man United side [in 1999] would beat the 1968 European Cup winners. He's got a point, because we're all over 50 now.
Nobby Stiles

I believe there are two Christs – him up there and me down here.
Hristo Stoichkov, *Bulgaria striker*

At school, Gazza used to put sweets down his socks and then give them to the teachers to eat.
Steve Stone

I said I'd timed my run into the box like David Platt, but the lads reckoned it was more like Gail Platt from *Coronation Street*.
Gavin Strachan *after scoring for Notts County*

If a Frenchman goes on about seagulls, trawlers and sardines, he's called a philosopher. I'd just be called a short Scottish bum talking crap.
Gordon Strachan

I kicked a few full-backs in my time but I always sent them flowers afterwards.
Mike Summerbee

The gaffer sent me to Liverpool to see if I could spot a weakness and I found one. The half-time tea's too milky.

Kevin Summerfield, *Shrewsbury player-coach, on their next FA Cup opponents*

[Being dropped] hasn't affected him. He's just too dopey and too thick to let things like that affect him.

Andrew Taylor, *Middlesbrough defender, on colleague David Wheater*

The boys have nicknamed me Ena Sharples because my head is forever in the net.

Ian Thain, *Keith goalkeeper, after conceding ten goals to Rangers in the Scottish Cup*

I don't mind Roy Keane making £60,000 a week. I made the same myself. The difference was I printed my own.

Mickey Thomas *after being jailed for counterfeiting money*

The Home Office won't let me go to Poland to play for Inter Cardiff in the UEFA Cup. As if I'd do a runner in Katowice.

Mickey Thomas *on playing again after leaving prison*

They weren't allowed to swap shirts with us because they'd got theirs from a supermarket when they arrived in Australia.

Archie Thompson, *Australia striker, after beating American Samoa 31-0*

When I went for a haircut in Dublin I asked for a Valderrama and they gave me a Val Doonican.

Andy Townsend

As the first bars of the Irish anthem ring out, I notice a TV camera zooming in. Should I move my lips and sing the two or three lines that I know?
Andy Townsend

I've never seen anything like the Old Trafford megastore. The queues to get in would fill Walsall's ground.
Andy Townsend

One manager told me that his midfield couldn't find me because I was standing still. I said that if they couldn't find me when I was stood still, how the hell did he expect them to find me if I was running around?
Roy Vernon, *ex-Everton and Wales forward, on finishing in non-league football*

When I drove a Jag with the windows blacked out, the Sheffield Wednesday lads called me The Pimp.
Chris Waddle

If I become a manager, first thing I'll do is buy a bottle of Grecian 2000.
Chris Waddle

That's the second time I've been sent off for celebrating. I'm going to staple my shirt on in future.
Ross Wallace, *Sunderland midfielder*

I played so badly that even my parents booed me off when I was substituted.

Theo Walcott *on England Under-21 duty*

Football matches are like days of the week. It can't be Sunday every day. There are also Mondays and Tuesdays.

George Weah

The only thing I have in common with George Best is that we come from the same place, played for the same club and were discovered by the same man.

Norman Whiteside

Our new Czech keeper Jan Stejskal only knows three words of English – 'my ball', 'away' and one other.

Ray Wilkins, *QPR team-mate*

Years later I asked George to stand in front of me so I could see his face. He asked why and I said, 'For years all I saw was your arse disappearing down the touchline.'

Graham Williams, *former West Brom full-back, who marked Best on his debut at 17*

I've gone in as emergency keeper three times now and conceded only one goal. Never mind me being 39 – I could play in goal until I'm 69.

Dean Windass

Roy Keane's worth every penny of the £54,000 a week they say he gets. It's a few bob more than me, give or take 49 grand.

Dean Windass

When the first foreign players came to Chelsea there was a book of Cockney rhyming slang going round. One day in a team meeting Ruud [Gullit] suddenly said: 'I'm a grave digger, and a very rich one.'

Dennis Wise

Obviously there's a language barrier at Chelsea. The majority of the lads speak Italian, but there's a few who don't.

Dennis Wise

I'm back at a proper football club. Mansfield Town have a lot of history. I'm older than Rushden & Diamonds.

Curtis Woodhouse

I had 11 clubs – 12 if you count Stringfellows.

Frank Worthington

I got the ball and the crowd started singing 'One Ronnie Corbett...'
Alan Wright, *diminutive Aston Villa defender*

I can't remember anything about my first-ever goal. It was against Oldham, Andy Goram was in goal, Alan Irvine crossed it for me and we won 3-2.
Ian Wright

If Dennis Bergkamp was in *Star Trek*, he'd be the best player in whatever solar system they were in.
Ian Wright

I must thank God for this success. Credit also goes to Steve Bruce.
Amir Zaki, *Wigan and Egypt striker*

I try to learn the language, but every time I go some place like Dennis Wise, my English go down.
Gianfranco Zola *at Chelsea*

Ninety-five per cent of my problems with the English language are the fault of that stupid little midget.
Gianfranco Zola *on Wise*

2: 'No knickers on': The managers

Lilian Nalis's goal was terrific. I've been trying to explain to him what the English word 'fluke' means.

Micky Adams, *Leicester manager*

I can't comment on the sending-off [of Dion Dublin] without sounding like Mr Wenger. It was a hot day and the sun was in my eyes.

Micky Adams, *Leicester manager*

My team looked like a woman who had a big fur coat on, but underneath she's got no knickers on.

Micky Adams *at Port Vale*

Compared with the Chelsea team that lost at Wigan, Port Vale resemble a woman in a big anorak stitched together from the pelts of mice.
Micky Adams *as reinterpreted by the* Guardian

This is probably the most prestigious match this club has ever played, but let's not big it up too much.
Tony Adams *before his Portsmouth side faced AC Milan*

It's football. It's fantastic. Unfortunately, the result is not fantastic.
Tony Adams *on Portsmouth's defeat by Liverpool, 24 hours before he was sacked*

I always take my notebook into the toilet to sketch out some match situations.
Dick Advocaat *at Rangers*

REPORTER: Someone got stabbed at West Ham v Millwall.
ALLARDYCE: That nearly happened to me at Millwall once – and I was playing for them.
Sam Allardyce, *Blackburn manager*

It's my birthday tomorrow so obviously that was an early Christmas present from the lads.
Sam Allardyce *after Blackburn beat Burnley*

In my first six months as Notts County manager, I had my name in chalk on the door.
Sam Allardyce

If you go shopping at Sainsbury's and ask for fillet steak, but don't have the money, you can't buy it. We've ended up with a gristly, old, fatty lump of lard up front, but at the moment he's tasting OK.

Martin Allen, *Cheltenham manager, on striker Julian Alsop*

I met Mick Jagger when I played for Oxford United and the Rolling Stones did a show there. Little did I know he'd be as famous as me one day.

Ron Atkinson

You're welcome to my phone number, gentlemen, but please remember not to ring me during *The Sweeney*.

Ron Atkinson *on becoming Manchester United manager*

Half an hour? You could shoot *Ben Hur* in half an hour. You've got 15 seconds.

Ron Atkinson *to a photographer who asked him for 30 minutes at United*

The way Valencia played, it's the first time we've had to replace divots in the players.

Ron Atkinson

Life's tough – I've had to swap my Merc for a BMW, I'm down to my last 37 suits and I'm drinking non-vintage champagne.

Ron Atkinson *after being sacked by United*

The only way I'd be interested in the England job is as player-manager.

Ron Atkinson *at Aston Villa*

We had a very constructive discussion at half-time, then decided to give it the full bollocks.

Ron Atkinson *at Aston Villa*

I know Cyrille Regis has found God. Now I want him to find the devil.

Ron Atkinson

It's bloody tough being a legend.

Ron Atkinson

I couldn't kick a ball as far as Carlton Palmer can trap it.

Ron Atkinson *at Sheffield Wednesday*

Gordon Strachan is 39 and there's no one fitter at his age, except maybe Raquel Welch.

Ron Atkinson

I am the best five-a-side player at Coventry. Mind you, that's probably why we're bottom of the Premiership.

Ron Atkinson

When I played a manager in *Dream Team* one of the scenes was me falling out with the chairman. I'm good at that.

Ron Atkinson

If that was a penalty, I'll plait sawdust.
Ron Atkinson

My missus reckons if people don't recognise me in the street, I go back and tell them who I am.
Ron Atkinson

When you're a manager you don't have fitted carpets.

John Barnwell *before being sacked by Walsall*

When you're a manager you're looking for good players, not blokes to marry your daughter.
Dave Bassett *on buying Vinnie Jones for Sheffield United*

Simon Tracey has got the brains of a rocking horse.
Dave Bassett *on his Sheffield United goalkeeper*

When I became Sheffield United manager, the board said there would be no money and they have kept their promise.
Dave Bassett

I ran out of petrol on the motorway. I phoned the police and they asked my name. I told them 'Dave Bassett'. This cop said, 'The Leicester manager?' I said yes and he burst out laughing.
Dave Bassett

I'd like to retire with half of what Cloughie has achieved and a quarter of his dough.

Dave Bassett

I was once called the spiv in a £400 suit. I felt right insulted. It cost at least a grand.

Dave Bassett

It's going to be my epitaph, isn't it? Deep in the shit, where he started.

Dave Bassett *facing relegation with Nottingham Forest*

Sam [Allardyce] was a ball-playing defender. He was always playing with your balls.

Dave Bassett

My aim as Cambridge United manager is to provide thrills with no frills, which isn't easy for a Cockney like me to say.

John Beck

Robbie [Fowler] taught me a new phrase because he said he was 'over the moon' to be back at Liverpool and I had never heard that before.

Rafael Benitez

I was watching a TV programme about accents the other day where they said the Birmingham dialect was the most difficult to understand, so I couldn't make out what they were saying.

Rafael Benitez on abuse he received from the Villa Park crowd

If Chelsea are naive and pure, then I'm Little Red Riding Hood.

Rafael Benitez

The second half was a crazy game and when it is a crazy game you can't control things. Why was it crazy? Because it was crazy.

Rafael Benitez after Liverpool drew at Wigan

I like having Xabi Alonso on the pitch because I can give him instructions so that the other manager can't understand.

Rafael Benitez, Liverpool manager

I want to dedicate this triumph to my dog, who died two years ago.

Carlos Bianchi, coach to Argentina's Boca Juniors, on winning the Treble

You wonder how someone could have come up with a plan straight out of *Blackadder*. You can picture Baldrick. 'I've got a cunning plan that'll take us further into debt.'

Kevin Blackwell, Leeds manager, on the free-spending Peter Ridsdale era

Even the ball-boys are 6ft 4in at Stoke.

Kevin Blackwell

Souey's a vain bastard – I thought he was going to tell me he was having another nose job, not open-heart surgery.

Phil Boersma, *Graeme Souness's No. 2 at Liverpool*

One minute you can be riding the crest of a wave and the next you're down. It's a funny old game. It's a great leveller and you can't get too cock-a-hoop about things. It's an old cliché but you have to take each game as it comes. In playing or management, you're only as good as your last game.

Billy Bonds *at West Ham*

If this game were a war, it would be America versus San Marino. In boxing it would be Muhammad Ali against Jimmy Krankie.

Aidy Boothroyd, *Watford manager, before playing Manchester United*

Q: Are funds available for new players?
A: Oh yes. About £2.54.

Ian Branfoot, *Fulham manager*

Can you believe my luck? Scotland get to the World Cup finals and the guy in charge wears a wig and has a nose that could cut a wedding cake.

Craig Brown, *Scotland No. 2, on manager Andy Roxburgh*

I once gave the Scotland players the afternoon off in Athens. One asked where there was to go. The hotel porter suggested the Acropolis and one of the lads said, 'I didn't know the discos were open in the afternoon.'

Craig Brown, *former Scotland manager*

When I played for Dundee, the manager was Bob Shankly, Bill's brother. I should have sensed the worst when he started positioning players for the squad photograph and told me, 'Just you sit at the end of the row, son. A pair of scissors will get rid of you.'

Craig Brown

Kevin [Keegan] and I have 63 international caps between us. He has 63 of them.

Craig Brown, *Scotland manager, before facing Keegan's England.*

Tony Woodcock? He's fast, strong, sharp and skilful, but otherwise he's useless.

Ken Brown, *Norwich manager*

Among those who rang me was Sir Alex Ferguson, who said you couldn't damage a face like mine.

Steve Bruce, *sporting a black eye from a scuffle with car thieves*

I told him: 'We're not interested in what's happened to you before – we just want you to reproduce what you did four years ago.'

Steve Bruce *on Henri Camara at Wigan*

Robbie [Savage] had to come off with cramp – in his hair.

Steve Bruce *at Birmingham*

Antonio Valencia is the best right-sided midfielder in the Premier League – if you put Cristiano Ronaldo on the left.
Steve Bruce *on Wigan's Ecuadorian winger*

People ask me the recipe for our success. Recipes are for cakes and pies.
Karel Brückner, *coach to the Czech Republic*

Did I put something of myself into the team? When we were playing well, yes. When we played shite, no.
Frank Burrows, *West Bromwich Albion caretaker manager*

I told the players I'd like them to win ugly, and that was the ugliest thing I've seen since the ugly sisters fell out of the ugly tree.
Terry Butcher *at Motherwell*

Towards the end I thought about bringing on my subs, Torvill and Dean.

Terry Butcher *on Dunfermline's plastic pitch*

It was a wonderful bit of individual skill and, if you saw it in La Liga, people would be waxing lyrical about it. Unfortunately because we have an ugly, ginger-haired centre-forward, we probably won't.
Colin Calderwood, *Nottingham Forest manager, about Joe Garner's 35-yard lob v Southampton*

We know it'll be very difficult against Motherwell because Mark McGhee and Scott Leitch are winners. They showed that last year by finishing third.
Jimmy Calderwood at Aberdeen

We weren't lucky – it was the Irish who had a flower up their backsides.

José Antonio Camacho, Spain coach

One of his cardinals introduced us, saying, 'This is Mr Charlton.' The Pope said, 'Ah yes, the boss.'
Jack Charlton at the Vatican in 1990 with the Ireland squad

We talked Alf [Ramsey] into letting us have a bit of sun by the hotel pool. He blew a whistle and we all lay down. Ten minutes later he blew again and we all turned over.
Jack Charlton on the 1970 World Cup

I might die being dragged down the River Tweed by a giant salmon, but not at a football match.
Jack Charlton

If Kevin Keegan fell into the Tyne, he'd come up with a salmon in his mouth.
Jack Charlton

Fergie's very supportive and understanding with fellow managers. Unless you beat him.

Frank Clark *at Manchester City*

You never say never because you never know what's round the corner.

Frank Clark *after leaving the Nottingham Forest job*

Towards the end at Forest I felt like a turkey waiting for Christmas.

Frank Clark

When we went abroad Fergie thought he could speak the lingo by adding an 'o' at the end of certain words. The fish was superbo, the meat was magnifico.

Neale Cooper, *Hartlepool manager and Aberdeen player under Alex Ferguson*

I've just signed another who doesn't speak English, so maybe my team talks will make sense now.

Steve Coppell *at Crystal Palace*

Liverpool's first goal was a foul, the second was offside and they'd never have scored the third if they hadn't got the other two.

Steve Coppell

I'm going to the pub in an area where you can't get any mobile reception.
Steve Coppell *on how to avoid selling Reading players on transfer-deadline day*

Their goal unsettled us, and no matter what you say at half-time, there's always that little bit of toothache in their minds.
Steve Coppell *at Reading*

As long as his brain is still active, he'll probably still be staggering out of the dugout in 2020.
Steve Coppell *on Sir Alex Ferguson*

It's just a game of football. There are 1.2 billion people in India who couldn't give a shit about what happened to Reading.
Steve Coppell *after defeat by Fulham*

I can't get inside my players' heads; one minute they're saving your life, the next they're breaking into your house and robbing your telly.
John Coleman, *Accrington Stanley manager*

Jimmy [Bullard] covered so much ground, I thought we had twins on the pitch.

Chris Coleman *at Fulham*

Football is like fighting a gorilla. You don't stop when you're tired. You stop when the gorilla is tired.
Chris Coleman *at Coventry*

If you took the goals out of it, I think it was pretty even.
Alan Curbishley, *West Ham manager, after losing 4-0 to Chelsea*

We went for a walk before the game and a bird dumped right on my head. They say that can be a lucky omen, and it was.
Simon Davey, *Barnsley manager, before an FA Cup win at Liverpool*

I just opened the trophy cabinet. Two Japanese soldiers came out.
Tommy Docherty *at Wolves*

We don't use a stopwatch for our Golden Goal competition. We use a calendar.
Tommy Docherty *at Wolves*

Preston offered me £10,000 to settle amicably. I told them they would have to be a lot more amicable than that.
Tommy Docherty *after another sacking*

I used to play for Preston, but then I've had more clubs than Jack Nicklaus.
Tommy Docherty

The Villa chairman, Doug Ellis, said he was right behind me. I told him I'd sooner have him in front of me where I could see him.
Tommy Docherty

I talk a lot. On any subject. Which is always football.

Tommy Docherty

Because of televising around the world, Jim Watt fought for the world title at two in the morning. That was to Jim's advantage – everybody fights at two in the morning in Glasgow.
Tommy Docherty

I was asked if I'd play a football manager in a TV play. I asked how long it would take. They said about ten days. I said: 'That's about par for the course.'
Tommy Docherty

Football's a rat race. And the rats are winning.
Tommy Docherty

I can't watch the long-ball teams. Football wasn't meant to be run by two linesmen and air-traffic control.
Tommy Docherty

Mark Wright would get an injury even if he went on *Question of Sport*.
Tommy Docherty *on England's injury-plagued centre-back*

When one door opens, another smashes you in the face.
Tommy Docherty *on being fired as Preston manager*

I told the back four: 'I'm glad you lot weren't defending me in my court case. The judge would have put his black cap on.'
Tommy Docherty *as Wolves manager*

Your pace is deceptive, son. You're even slower than you look.

Tommy Docherty *to Leighton James*

Half a million for Remi Moses? You could get the original Moses and the tablets for that price.
Tommy Docherty

I told my players it's not possible to play football with your pants full.
Ernst Dokupil, *Rapid Vienna coach, after defeat by Manchester United*

My players reckon I look like [former Dead Or Alive singer] Pete Burns. I don't know who he is, but he's obviously not blessed with good looks.
Iain Dowie *at Crystal Palace*

There's not much you can do to stop Brian Laudrup, other than sending a couple of chaps in balaclavas with baseball bats round to his house.
Jim Duff, *Hibernian manager*

My grandmother never understood you could be paid so much for kicking a ball. So every time I see her she slips me £5 or £10.

Sven-Göran Eriksson, *England manager*

INTERVIEWER: How would you like to leave the England job?
ERIKSSON: Alive.

Sven-Göran Eriksson *in a 2006 TV interview*

I always enjoy the summer. You can't lose any matches.

Roy Evans, *Liverpool manager*

We had one director who wanted us to sign Salford Van Hire because he thought he was a Dutch international.

Fred Eyre, *former Wigan Athletic assistant manager*

If Gary Neville was an inch taller he'd be the best centre-half in Britain. His dad is 6ft 2in. I'd check the milkman.

Alex Ferguson

It would have been Sir Matt Busby's 90th birthday today [when Manchester United won the Champions League final in 1999]. All I know is someone was doing an awful lot of kicking up there.

Alex Ferguson

Being made a freeman of Glasgow means I'm allowed to hang my washing on Glasgow Green. And if I'm ever arrested in the city, I'm entitled to my own cell, which could come in handy.

Alex Ferguson

Steve McClaren's first game as United coach was an 8-1 win at Nottingham Forest. I told him afterwards: 'We're looking for some improvement.'
Sir Alex Ferguson *after his former No. 2 became England manager*

There were only three tackles on [José Antonio] Reyes. That hardly constitutes the *Texas Chainsaw Massacre*.
Sir Alex Ferguson *after a Manchester United v Arsenal match*

The boy [Wes Brown] has had two cruciates and a broken ankle. Everyone at the club is praying he gets a break.
Sir Alex Ferguson

When an Italian says it's pasta I check under the sauce to make sure. They're the inventors of the smokescreen.
Sir Alex Ferguson

The title race is getting really tight now. I call it squeaky-bum time.

Sir Alex Ferguson

Christ almighty, I wouldn't sell Real Madrid a virus, let alone Cristiano Ronaldo.
Sir Alex Ferguson

Schmeichel was towering over me and the other lads covered their eyes. I looked up and thought, If he does hit me, I'm dead.
Sir Alex Ferguson

Gary Neville was having a piss at the training ground one day, by a fence. From 45 yards, Paul Scholes whacked him right in the arse.
Sir Alex Ferguson

For us to get a penalty we need a certificate from the Pope and a personal letter from the Queen.
Sir Alex Ferguson

Marriage helps footballers. It settles them down – and you know where they are.

Sir Alex Ferguson on Wayne Rooney

The transfer market's so dead I've been phoning myself and disguising my voice just for a bit of interest.
Gerry Francis, QPR manager

I have to laugh when I see Harry [Redknapp] spending millions at Tottenham. When I was manager there, I had to lend *them* money.
Gerry Francis

There were 47 players when I arrived and 49 when I found two more in a cupboard.
Trevor Francis after succeeding Barry Fry as Birmingham manager

When I first became a manager, with Dunstable, attendances were so low we used to tell the team the crowd changes.
Barry Fry

I got arrested one Christmas Day driving a tractor to flatten the pitch. I told the policeman who I was and he said, 'Oh yeah, and I'm Georgie Best.'
Barry Fry at Barnet

Q: If you won the Lottery, what would you buy?
A: 27 new strikers.
Barry Fry at Birmingham

Terry Venables is a great tactician, which is something I admire because I don't do tactics.
Barry Fry

Kirstine's out shopping as usual. I'm down the Job Centre looking for employment. Funny old game, innit?
Barry Fry's answerphone message after Birmingham sacked him

I no longer run down the touchline when we score. I just waddle a bit.
Barry Fry at Peterborough

Any more defeats and Barry Fry the owner will have to call in that useless sod Barry Fry the manager and tell him: 'It's on yer bike, son.'
Barry Fry *on his dual role at Peterborough*

If I got as many points for football as for my driving offences, I'd be in the Premiership by now.
Barry Fry, *Jaguar driver*

I almost dived on the telly when I saw Joe come on. I nearly had a third heart attack.
Barry Fry *after Peterborough goalkeeper Joe Lewis was sent on to play up front for England Under-21s*

The players are under no pressure to get a result, so you never know what might happen.
Tommy Gemmell, *Albion Rovers manager, before losing 11-0 to Partick Thistle*

How do you defend against the Eiffel Tower?

Jelle Goes, *Estonia coach, after Peter Crouch headed a goal for England against his team*

Grow your hair and you'll be considered for England.

John Gorman, *Glenn Hoddle's No. 2, to shaven-headed Julian Dicks*

My manager at Wolves, Bill McGarry, told me: 'If I see you in our half, I'll kick your arse.' It was music to my ears.

Bobby Gould *on being a striker in the 1970s*

There was a demo against me, but it's not the worst reception I've ever had. Did you ever see me as a player?

Bobby Gould *as West Brom manager*

I went to see Stuart Pearce play for Wealdstone on a stinking night at Yeovil. After ten minutes he put in a thundering tackle and the winger landed in my wife's lap. I said to her: 'That's it. I've seen enough. I'm going home.'

Bobby Gould *on how he came to sign Pearce for Coventry*

A broken nose is nothing – I tried to get one throughout my playing career because it adds character to your face.

George Graham *after Arsenal's Andy Linighan headed the FA Cup final winner with a broken nose*

Does it surprise you [Mourinho] opened his mouth? You go to a restaurant, you know why the fish is on the table? Because it opened its mouth.

Avram Grant

I am not the Special One. I'm the Normal One. But my wife says I am special. What am I like? I am 180cm.
Avram Grant

We've got people at Aston Villa who like wearing dresses and having their bottoms spanked, so Paul [Merson] should fit in well.
John Gregory

We were wimpish – and wanky, like they say in *Men Behaving Badly*.
John Gregory *after a Villa defeat*

You're always just one defeat from a crisis. On that basis, we're in deep shit.

John Gregory *after two defeats for Villa*

The lads have already nicknamed him Horse, but I'm not going into details.
Bryan Gunn, *Norwich manager, on new signing Grant Holt*

There are only two certainties in life: people die and football managers get the sack.
Eoin Hand, *Republic of Ireland manager*

We're now arithmetically, not mathematically, safe from relegation. There's neither algebra nor geometry involved in the calculations.
Tom Hendrie, *St Mirren manager*

Wales gave us a difficult game. For five or six minutes.

Guus Hiddink, *Holland manager, after a 7-1 win*

I don't know the words of the Russia national anthem, but I like the melody very much so I'll hum along. When I'm a traitor, I like to be a very good traitor.

Guus Hiddink, *Russia's Dutch coach, before beating Holland*

We came back from the dead. Well, it is Easter Monday.

Glenn Hoddle *after Swindon came from 4-1 down to beat Birmingham*

Even the Pope would think twice about taking the England manager's job.

Roy Hodgson, *Switzerland manager*

I keep hearing people say, 'You've got to laugh, haven't you?' Tommy Cooper, Monty Python and Frasier combined couldn't have got me laughing on the bus back from Middlesbrough.

Roy Hodgson *at Blackburn*

Andy Johnson was literally banjoed out of the game by a player who made no attempt to win the ball.

Roy Hodgson *at Fulham*

We were like the Dog & Duck in the first half and Real Madrid in the second.

Ian Holloway *at QPR*

I'm sick of every Tom, Dick and Harry getting linked with my job every day. Well, ding dang doo. It's my job. I own it.

Ian Holloway shortly before being ousted by QPR

I went swimming with my players but my trunks were so tight that I got called a budgie-smuggler.

Ian Holloway at Plymouth

We threw everything at them – kitchen sink, golf clubs, emptied the garage. It wasn't enough but at least my garage is tidy now.

Ian Holloway at Plymouth

When you're a manager it's a case of have suitcase will travel. And I certainly didn't want to travel with my trousers down.

Ian Holloway

Getting to the last eight of the FA Cup, I'm like a badger at the start of the pairing-up season.

Ian Holloway at Plymouth

Strikers are very much like postmen – they have to get in and out before the dog starts to have a go.

Ian Holloway

I was a bit worried no one was going to turn up at my book signing. I was relieved to see some people there. I thought about sitting outside Northern Rock because there would be a queue there.

Ian Holloway

If you go to the ballet you have about eight intervals – it's different class. In fact you could almost have your ten pints during the breaks and by the end of it you're loving it. I strongly recommend it.
Ian Holloway

I was never tempted to become a punk. I was always as smooth as a cashmere codpiece.
Ian Holloway

It's a football club, not a prison. People shouldn't see me coming and think, Oh, here's that bastard.
Ian Holloway *at Leicester*

If that was a penalty, I'll call myself Alec McJockstrap and put on a kilt.

Ian Holloway *after Leicester conceded a penalty at Ipswich*

I'd have put my house, its contents, my entire wardrobe, my undergarments, my socks and my shoes on the fact that he would score. How he didn't, I have no idea.
Ian Holloway *on a miss by Leicester's Iain Hume*

We've got to go to Stoke and tweak the nose of fear and stick an ice cube down the T-shirt of terror. That's not me talking, it's Blackadder.
Ian Holloway *before Leicester's relegation*

[Enrique] De Lucas's pedigree is unbelievable. If he were a dog he'd win Crufts.

Ian Holloway, *Blackpool manager*

Everyone needs to work, whether you're a flamboyant striker or a run-of-the-mill midfielder like I was. Some are piano carriers who pick it up, put it on the stage, let the pianist sit down and play it. But without them there would be no piano on stage.

Ian Holloway *at Blackpool*

I love Blackpool. We're very similar. We both look better in the dark.

Ian Holloway

If you're a burglar, it's no good poncing about outside somebody's house, looking good with your swag bag ready. Just get in there, burgle them, and come out. I don't advocate that obviously. It's just an analogy.

Ian Holloway *after Blackpool lost to Crystal Palace*

It was a game of two halves and we were crap in both of them.

Brian Horton, *Oxford manager*

George Graham running a nightclub? Yes. A football club? Absolutely not.

Don Howe, *former Arsenal coach, recalls Graham the player*

In the end we lost a bad third goal because of an individual error by the goalkeeper, but I'm not going to point the finger of blame at anyone for that.

John Hughes, *Falkirk manager*

Since I arrived at the club I've been walking around with my slippers on, but now the gloves are off.

John Hughes *after taking over at Hibernian*

I've given one player carte blanche, as Ron Greenwood used to say, though I didn't use that phrase in the dressing room. Told him to go where he liked.

Geoff Hurst *as Telford United player-manager*

Sometimes you want to crack open the champagne, other times you want to kick the dog.

Paul Ince *at Macclesfield*

Andrew O'Brien has got a big hooter. Some of the strikers he marks go off with broken elbows.

Paul Jewell *at Bradford City*

With me and Iain Dowie on the touchline it could turn into a beauty contest.

Paul Jewell *at Derby*

It would be easy to say that losing Alan Stubbs to injury made all the difference. Obviously it didn't, but it did make a hell of a difference.

Paul Jewell *after Derby lost 6-1 to Chelsea*

I've got more points on my driving licence than Derby have got in the Premier League.

Paul Jewell *as Derby faced relegation with a record-low 11 points*

He's six foot two, brave as a lion, strong as an ox and quick as lightning. If he was good looking, you'd say he has everything.

Paul Jewell *on Cristiano Ronaldo*

I could be on the list to take over at Rangers, but only until they find out what school I went to.

Paul Jewell

My mum bought me a pair of 'lucky' underpants. I'm not saying whether I'm wearing them, but I hope I don't get knocked down by a bus on the way home.

Gary Johnson *at Bristol City*

Some of the players got handbags for Christmas and were anxious to show them off.

Gary Johnson *after a fracas between Bristol City and Crystal Palace players*

When I first came to Cardiff City we used to train in what we called Dogshit Park.

Dave Jones *at Cardiff*

Stoke City have fantastic potential – it's a sleeping monster.
Chris Kamara

I might have to start persuading players that Sunderland is closer to London than it actually is.
Roy Keane *claiming that players' wives talked them into joining London clubs rather than Sunderland*

If you're driving to work, don't get in the car with Liam Miller because he has more car crashes than anyone I know.
Roy Keane *on the Sunderland midfielder's habit of arriving late for training*

Maybe I will get a chance to give my views to the FA, but last time they had a murder lawyer against me, so it could be a hard case to win.
Roy Keane *on an FA misconduct charge*

If they wanted the players smiling all the time they should have employed Roy Chubby Brown rather than me.

Roy Keane *after leaving Sunderland*

We should never have allowed [Coventry's] Clinton Morrison to stoop so low to score his second. When it comes in at that height you take his head off.
Roy Keane, *Ipswich manager*

If anyone ever hears that Kevin Keegan is coming back to English football, they can laugh as much as I will. It will never happen.

Kevin Keegan in 1985 on leaving to live in Spain

Sir John [Hall] was a multi-millionaire when I joined Newcastle. Now he's just an ordinary millionaire.

Kevin Keegan after buying Alan Shearer for £15m

David Ginola has just handed in a transfer request. The handwriting was beautiful.

Kevin Keegan

People say you need coaching badges to be a manager, but when I went to Newcastle my only qualification was a thousand rounds of golf in Spain.

Kevin Keegan

Scholesy, go out there and drop a few hand grenades.

Kevin Keegan as England manager. Paul Scholes was promptly sent off against Sweden

Kevin Phillips was so keen to join up with England that he almost got here early enough to meet the last squad going home.

Kevin Keegan

Some parts of the England manager's job I did very well, but not the key part of getting players to win football matches.
Kevin Keegan

Danny Tiatto is not going to make a mistake on purpose.
Kevin Keegan *at Manchester City*

The only way we'll get into Europe is by ferry.
Kevin Keegan *after returning as Newcastle manager*

Welcome to the Grey Hair Club.
Kevin Keegan *to John Aldridge when he became Tranmere manager*

I went over to see Robbie in Liverpool, risked getting my tyres and wheels nicked to speak to him.
Kevin Keegan, *Manchester City manager*

Portsmouth have got their eyes on fifth place and one eye on the FA Cup final.
Kevin Keegan

The transfer market has changed because of the Bosnian ruling.

Joe Kinnear

As a manager you can get sacked for farting in the wrong direction.
Joe Kinnear

The players can wear jeans and earrings for all I care. But I draw the line at stockings and suspenders, at least until after the match.
Joe Kinnear *relaxes Wimbledon predecessor Peter Withe's dress code*

I'm out at the moment, but if you're chairman of Barcelona, Real Madrid or AC Milan, I'll get straight back to you. The rest can wait.
Joe Kinnear *– between jobs – on his answerphone message*

I'm like a new stranger to the players.
Joe Kinnear *arrives at Newcastle*

Shay [Given] pulled out with a knee injury as did Insomnia... Insomnia... er, Charlie.

Joe Kinnear, *Newcastle manager, renames Charles N'Zogbia*

Charles [N'Zogbia] is a mixed-up kid who needs to grow up. Oh, and his agent is full of shit.
Joe Kinnear *when N'Zogbia promptly asked for a transfer*

I could have put four f*****g pigeons in midfield and they would have played better.
John Lambie, *Partick Thistle manager*

TRAINER: McGlashan's concussed, gaffer, and doesn't know who he is.
LAMBIE: That's great – tell him he's Pelé and get him back on.
John Lambie in an exchange during a Partick fixture

If you see that your team plays this shit like we did in the first half, you can just run out of the stadium and say 'it's Mother's Day tomorrow' and forget about the football. But we are guys, we are at Ibrox and we are still in the first half. I wanted to kill some of the people in my dressing room at half-time, but then I have to go to jail and we don't get a point! But the second half was sexy.
Csaba László, Hearts manager

It doesn't matter if it's Christmas Day or Mother's Day, we hand out gifts. Now it's Easter, we gave away a huge egg after 30 seconds.
Csaba László at Hearts

We have the chances with Andy Driver. OK, I don't like to name names, but this is the difference with the player who plays in the Champions League: he comes, he scores, he takes his Ferrari and goes and looks for the nice girls. And we get in our Skodas and Citroens and go home from Falkirk with one point.
Csaba László at Hearts

The last time Grimsby were top of the First Division, dinosaurs roamed the earth.
Lennie Lawrence in 2001

The pitch was very sandy, like a beach. I never realised Lincoln was a seaside town.
Brian Laws, *Scunthorpe manager*

People keep on about stars and flair. For me, you find stars in the sky and flair at the bottom of your trousers.
Gordon Lee *at Everton*

Someone stole my bike four weeks ago. It felt terrible and it felt the same again today because we were robbed.
Craig Levein, *Dundee United manager, after a draw with Falkirk*

I've kicked bottles of water, bags and shoes in the dressing room many times, but I've never hit a player. The Scots must have superior technique.
Marcello Lippi, *Juventus coach, after Alex Ferguson kicked a boot which cut David Beckham's face*

Before City got their first we could have been 3-0 up. I said to my physio: 'I'm going to have a cigar. If we keep this up we'll get double figures.'
Malcolm Macdonald, *Huddersfield manager, after a 10-1 defeat at Manchester City*

We were forced to play so many youngsters that you had to burp and wind them after each game.

Mick McCarthy *at Millwall*

I asked the players who wanted to take a penalty in the shoot-out. There was an awful smell coming from some of them.
Mick McCarthy *at Millwall*

I met a pal who'd lost track of me and asked what I was doing. I said I was player-manager of Millwall. His wife immediately said: 'How embarrassing.'
Mick McCarthy

I told the Millwall chairman that if he ever wants to sack me, all he has to do is take me into town, buy me a meal, a few pints and a cigar and I'll piss off.
Mick McCarthy

Anyone who uses the word 'quintessentially' in a half-time talk is talking crap.

Mick McCarthy, *Republic of Ireland manager, on Niall Quinn*

No regrets, none at all. My only regret is that we went out on penalties. That's my only regret. But no, no regrets.
Mick McCarthy *after the Republic's exit from the 2002 World Cup*

My reaction when I was offered the chance to become Sunderland manager? Yee-ha!
Mick McCarthy

It wasn't a monkey on my back. It was more like *Planet of the Apes*.
Mick McCarthy *after his Sunderland team ended a long winless run*

That was a cross – if he meant it as a shot, I'll drop my trousers in Burton's window.

Mick McCarthy *alleging an 'accidental' goal by Swindon*

A greyhound is going through a field and he sees a rabbit. The rabbit gets up and starts running. The greyhound fancies a bit of snap but the rabbit fancies his life. Who runs the harder? The rabbit, absolutely. That's been my view on life.
Mick McCarthy *at Wolves*

There's two scenarios here. It's an anagram, isn't it? If I get promoted I'm a god and if we don't I'm a dog.
Mick McCarthy *at Wolves*

I've not got carried away all season, so I won't start jumping up and down waving my knickers in the air now.
Mick McCarthy *about to clinch promotion with Wolves*

I'd have backed him to put the penalty away, but I wouldn't put my house on anyone scoring. Not when I broke my bollocks to pay for my mortgage.
Mick McCarthy *after Wolves' Sylvan Ebanks-Blake missed a vital penalty*

People say beating Birmingham [in the FA Cup] will give us a psychological advantage in the promotion race, but I don't believe in all that mumbo-jumbo bollocks.
Mick McCarthy at Wolves

Backsides and opinions, we've all got them, but it's not always a good idea to air them in public.
Mick McCarthy on Roy Keane's decision to leave Sunderland

I am fat. It's not difficult to get that way with my lifestyle, but the important thing is that it doesn't affect my golf swing.
Mark McGhee at Wolves on the taunts against him by Reading fans

The fans at Millwall presented me with an enamel badge and the words 'Cheer Up Mark McGhee'. They thought I was a miserable bastard.

Mark McGhee

LOUIS EDWARDS (MANCHESTER UNITED CHAIRMAN): We've received more than 30 applications for the post of Manchester United manager.
MCGUINNESS: Yes, and I wrote all of them.
Wilf McGuinness at the press conference to unveil him as Matt Busby's successor

The chairman called me into his office and said: 'Wilf, I don't know how we'd manage without you, but we're going to try.'
Wilf McGuinness

Ron Atkinson was one of the best half-backs in the country. What a pity he had to play his football in the town.
Wilf McGuinness

The match against Arshenal isch big newsch in Englisch media.
Steve McClaren, *Twente Enschede manager, injects a Dutch accent into an interview*

For what Stoke offered us for Peter Thorne, you couldn't even get a decent pie lady.
Steve McMahon *at Swindon*

We climbed three mountains and then proceeded to throw ourselves off them.
Billy McNeill, *Celtic manager*

If players don't want to get kicked, they should become accountants.

Roberto Mancini, *Inter Milan coach*

We signed Jason Koumas because we haven't got his type of player – someone who can pass and score goals.
Gary Megson, *West Brom manager*

Jason Roberts? When he put in a transfer request, he spelt his own name wrong.
Gary Megson

A football manager has about the same sort of job security as a kamikaze pilot.
Gary Megson *at Bolton*

I wasn't surprised Nic wanted to take Chelsea's offer – we were only paying him two dead frogs and a conker.
Gary Megson *on Nicolas Anelka's departure from Bolton*

If someone in the crowd spits at you, you've just got to swallow it.
Gordon Milne, *Leicester manager*

Liverpool fans continue to sing 'You've got no history' to us. We continue to make it.
José Mourinho *at Chelsea*

As we say in Portugal, Spurs brought the bus and left it in front of the goal.

José Mourinho *at Chelsea*

During the afternoon it rained only inside Blackburn's stadium. That place has its own micro-climate.
José Mourinho *at Chelsea*

My wife is in Portugal with the dog. So the city of London is safe – the big threat is away.
José Mourinho

I had a glass of wine and spent half an hour with Sir Alex after the game. I told him Inter's tactics and he gave me United's starting 11.
José Mourinho *on a scouting trip to Old Trafford before their clubs met in the Champions League*

Now they say in England that [Carlo] Ancelotti is Prince Charles. But I know only one Prince Charles and that is the Prince of Wales.
José Mourinho

I'm not wearing Mr Wenger glasses. I really didn't get a good view of the incident.

Tony Mowbray *at West Bromwich Albion*

PRESS STEWARD: Ladies and gentlemen, the West Brom manager.
MOWBRAY: You don't know my name, do you?
STEWARD: No.
Tony Mowbray *after a Burnley v Albion FA Cup tie*

I'd hang myself, but the club can't afford the rope.
Iain Munro, *Hamilton Academical manager*

No one can work miracles and that applies to people like Holmes and Watson, the Marx Brothers, Bilko, Inspector Clouseau or Winston Churchill. All these had immeasurable qualities but I don't know whether any of them had the attributes to win promotion for Lincoln City.

Colin Murphy, *Lincoln manager, in his programme column*

Watching Man City is probably the best laxative you can take.

Phil Neal, *City caretaker manager*

We had a difference of opinion. I thought I was brilliant, he didn't.

Martin O'Neill *on Brian Clough at Nottingham Forest*

When Forest's England players went off on international duty, Cloughie used to say, 'Don't get injured.' When I went off with Northern Ireland, all he said to me was, 'Don't come back.'

Martin O'Neill

I asked Cloughie, 'Why am I playing for the second team?' He said, 'Because you're too good for the thirds.'

Martin O'Neill

No one gave us a chance of surviving in the Premiership except for some paper in Bulgaria that said we'd stay up. I'm going to write and thank him.

Martin O'Neill *at Leicester*

Gerry Taggart likes to think he came to Leicester under the Bosman ruling, but that's just another way of saying free transfer.
Martin O'Neill

If the players are looking for a sign from me, I'm sorry but I'll be in the toilet somewhere.
Martin O'Neill *before Celtic v Porto in the UEFA Cup final*

When they scored their third I actually thought they'd gone off into Seville to celebrate.
Martin O'Neill *on Porto's long, time-wasting goal celebrations*

Being manager is hard enough without going on the board and having to decide whether to sack myself or not.
Martin O'Neill *after declining a Celtic directorship*

Although I love it, I'm particularly hopeless at golf. My handicap? Severe.

Martin O'Neill *at Aston Villa*

Once Ashley [Young] puts on some weight he'll be fantastic. Right now he's about three and a half stone. A couple of times we've put him through the letterbox.
Martin O'Neill *at Villa*

Big clubs do get the decisions from referees. I want to make Aston Villa a big club so we get them too.
Martin O'Neill

We've lost 11 in a row, but things change. Who's to say I won't be England manager in ten years' time?
Carlton Palmer *at Stockport*

The gaffer thought Liverpol were the sort of club who put things in your tea. He used to tell us: 'Don't drink it. The cheating bastards probably put something in it.' At Anfield, he wouldn't drink anything that wasn't sealed.
Stuart Pearce *on Brian Clough*

Our problem isn't keeping the players out of the nightclubs, it's getting them out of the banks.
Paul Philipp, *Luxembourg coach, on his team of bank clerks and insurance agents*

Our central defenders, Gary Doherty and Anthony Gardner, were fantastic and I told them that when they go to bed tonight they should think of each other.
David Pleat *at Tottenham*

At Bournemouth, we once went to Grimsby and Luther Blissett turned up in a magnificent cream suit, black shirt and cream tie. We were 3-0 down at half-time and Harry smashed a cup of tea which went all over Luther's suit.
Tony Pulis, *Stoke manager, recalls playing under Harry Redknapp*

We made an offer to Milan for Kaka and it was turned down. We offered Stoke-on-Trent.

Tony Pulis

Our groundsman is fitter than some of my players.

Jimmy Quinn, *Swindon manager*

If I'm alone on the road in England I begin to question whether I'm on the right side of the road. When I go back to Italy I've started to wonder the same thing. It's confusing.

Claudio Ranieri *at Chelsea*

If it is just the case that you need a first XI and three or four more players, then why did Christopher Columbus sail to India to discover America?

Claudio Ranieri *at Chelsea*

A football manager is like a parachutist. At times it doesn't open and you splatter on the ground. In England it is an umbrella. You understand, Mary Poppins?

Claudio Ranieri

My team is like an orchestra. To play the symphony correctly I need the boom-boom but also the tweet-tweet. Sometimes the boom and the tweet go well together.

Claudio Ranieri *at Chelsea*

The 'Save Ranieri' campaign in the *Evening Standard* is flattering save for one thing. They can't run a picture of me in my glasses. Gladiators don't wear glasses in the Colosseum.

Claudio Ranieri *shortly before leaving Chelsea*

I've got coaching badges but they came out of a cornflakes packet.

Harry Redknapp *at West Ham*

John Hartson has got more previous than Jack the Ripper.

Harry Redknapp *at West Ham*

I told my chairman that David O'Leary paid £18m for Rio Ferdinand and Leeds have given him £5m in share options. I bring in £18m and all I get is a bacon sandwich.

Harry Redknapp *at West Ham*

Even though we had Moore, Hurst and Peters, West Ham's average finish was about 17th. Which shows how crap the other eight of us were.

Harry Redknapp, *former Hammers player*

We were all on the coach waiting to go to Stockport and [Florin] Raducioiu was in Harvey Nichols shopping with his missus.

Harry Redknapp *at West Ham*

If I'd got caught shagging my secretary, I wouldn't be able to come to work. I'd go away and hide.

Harry Redknapp *after being arrested on corruption charges*

There's a new system to do transfers on the internet, but I can't even work my video, so it'll be no use to me.

Harry Redknapp

I've just been given a video of the game and I'm going to record *Neighbours* over it.

Harry Redknapp

I told my players that Frank Lampard has got 17 goals from midfield this season, but they just said, 'That's why he's on 150 grand a week.'

Harry Redknapp *at Portsmouth*

We're going to Nigeria in pre-season. Don't tell the lads that yet. They might have lost the FA Cup if I'd told 'em.

Harry Redknapp *after Portsmouth won the FA Cup*

I should get out now – I've taken this team as far as I can.

Harry Redknapp *after five wins out of his six with his new club, Tottenham*

Not speaking English is a problem. You've always got his interpreter running around the training ground. Sometimes you pass the ball through the middle and he chases it. And the interpreter is running alongside him and he gets in there and heads it into the net.

Harry Redknapp *on Tottenham's Russian striker Roman Pavlyuchenko*

Knowing Rio as I do, having to do drug tests would have got up his nose.
Harry Redknapp

The lads have just heard the replay at Kilmarnock is being televised, so they'll be getting a haircut and getting the fake tan on.
Brian Reid, *Ayr United manager*

Mr Wenger is a very clever man, but I have to say that what he said is crap.
Peter Reid, *Sunderland manager, after a game with Arsenal*

I'm the only man in Athens who is allowed to drive in the bus lane.
Otto Rehhagel, *coach to Greece, on their triumph at Euro 2004*

We need to become killers at the back, in the nicest possible way.
Brendan Rodgers, *Watford manager*

The ball hit a water sprinkler and shot high into the air. It was purely an instinctive reaction when Richard Gough grabbed the ball as it flew over his head.

Andy Roxburgh, *Scotland manager, after his captain was sent off against Switzerland*

Further to your recent letter, I am sorry we cannot help you in your search for academics. In fact two of the back four cannot read.

Joe Royle, *Oldham manager, replying to a reporter researching footballers with degrees*

Should they give Fergie the England job? Of course. Give the rest of us a bloomin' chance.

Joe Royle *at Everton*

The plan is to get out of management while I've still got all my marbles and my hair.

Joe Royle *at Everton*

I'm told that David Ginola ran up the tunnel and dived in the bath.

Joe Royle

I'm just glad the referees can't understand what he's saying to them.

Joe Royle *on Duncan Ferguson at Everton*

I may be a Scouser but I'm not stupid.

Joe Royle *at Manchester City*

I may have been the captain when we went down, but not when we hit the iceberg.

Joe Royle *on relegation with Manchester City*

To score four when you're playing like pigs in labour is fantastic.
Joe Royle *at Manchester City*

I've done 16 years at Port Vale. Even the Great Train Robbers didn't get that long.
John Rudge

I do not sleep with [Didier] Drogba. Where he was last night? I don't know – I'm not his policeman.
Luiz Felipe Scolari *on reports that the Chelsea striker had met Inter Milan*

He plays the ball better with his hands than his foot – it's fantastic!
Luiz Felipe Scolari *on Rory Delap's long throw-ins for Stoke*

Rab Douglas is feeling a calf but he's not causing concern.

Jocky Scott, *Dundee manager*

I expect the Croats to come... oh dear, I'd better not say fighting, had I?
Peter Shreeves, *Tottenham manager, before playing Hajduk Split during the war in former Yugoslavia*

Glenn [Hoddle] has a very tough persona, despite the fact that they used to call him Glenda.
Peter Shreeves, *ex-Tottenham manager*

There are 0-0 draws and 0-0 draws, and this was a 0-0 draw.

John Sillett, Coventry manager

We've lost seven games 1-0 and drawn seven 0-0. If we'd drawn the ones we lost 1-0, we'd have another seven points and if the seven goalless draws had been 1-0 to us we'd have 28 points more and be third in the Premiership.

Alan Smith, Crystal Palace manager, en route to relegation

[Trevor] Francis told me he had a system for taking penalties. I don't know what it is but it's obviously bloody useless.

Jim Smith, QPR manager, after Francis's second successive miss

Gullit going isn't a shock but Vialli taking over is. They've obviously gone for continuity because Chelsea's players can only understand broken English.

Jim Smith at Derby

At Derby, Stefano Eranio could stop the ball dead with his toe. At half-time one day he said to our big, ugly centre-half Spencer Prior: 'Why you always put ball in stand? No players in stand.'

Jim Smith

We're going to make sure everybody has to have haggis and porridge in the canteen from now on.

Walter Smith, Everton manager, on the club's sizeable Scottish element

He always tries to have a good relationship with his managers and if you're going to leave he always sacks you nicely.

Walter Smith *on Rangers' chairman Sir David Murray*

At Liverpool, Bob Paisley once pinned a map on the wall and never said a single word to us. 'Just take a look at that,' he said.

Graeme Souness

Pressure? Sitting at home, watching *Coronation Street* with slippers on. I'd find that very stressful.

Graeme Souness *at Liverpool*

Eyal [Berkovic] is Jewish and I'm Scottish so it will be hard for us to reach a financial agreement.

Graeme Souness *at Blackburn*

I haven't seen him yet to say congratulations – I think he is on an open-top bus in Redcar.

Gareth Southgate, *Middlesbrough manager, when defender David Wheater was picked by England*

I've got a diploma in Business Studies but that won't be any use – I've headed too many footballs since then.

Nigel Spackman *on becoming Sheffield United manager*

Fergie was one for coming out with the strangest of things. A couple of Fergieisms were 'Have you ever seen a Pakistani funeral?' or 'Have you ever seen an Italian with a cold?'
Pat Stanton, *Sir Alex's assistant at Aberdeen*

Never play tennis with George [Boateng] because he cheats. Every time he hits a winner he thanks the Lord, so it's always two against one.
Gordon Strachan *at Coventry*

Have you seen the size of the house he owns in Leicester? He owns half of Leicester and won't want to leave that behind.
Gordon Strachan *before Coventry lost Gary McAllister to Liverpool*

We don't get penalties at Coventry. If an opposition defender cut the head off one of my players with a machete, dug a hole and buried it, then we might. Otherwise no.
Gordon Strachan

The world looks a totally different place after you've won. I can even enjoy watching *Blind Date* or laugh at *Noel's House Party*.
Gordon Strachan *at Coventry*

If you don't know what's going on, start waving your arms about as if you do.

Gordon Strachan *on football management*

[Fabien] Barthez sat in my office smoking during the second half. Comes off for ill health and puts a fag in his mouth. It was a no-smoking area too.

Gordon Strachan, *Southampton manager, after the Manchester United keeper was substituted at The Dell*

Marians Pahars has also caught every virus going, bar a computer virus. And he's working on that even now.

Gordon Strachan *at Southampton*

When you go to Anfield or Old Trafford it pays not to wear a coloured shirt. I always wear a white one so no one can see the sweat stains as the pressure mounts.

Gordon Strachan

There's a lot of ice in that dressing room – it's like the dining room on the *Titanic* in there.

Gordon Strachan, *Celtic manager, after a bruising encounter at Hearts*

It's dangerous to try to fight him [Alex Ferguson] when you've got a sponge and he's armed with a machine gun.

Gordon Strachan *at Celtic*

He is not a bad lad. If it said 'God bless Myra Hindley', I might have a problem.

Gordon Strachan *after Celtic keeper Artur Boruc's 'God bless the Pope' T-shirt incensed Rangers fans*

We Scots owe the English big time. They stole our land, our oil, perpetrated the Highland Clearances and now they've even pinched Billy Connolly.

Gordon Strachan

You can call me a turnip, but don't ever call me Gordon.

Graham Taylor, *former England manager*

Every manager gets sacked, but it's better to be sacked by Real Madrid than anyone else.

John Toshack

I haven't seen a Real Madrid side this bad since I managed them.

John Toshack *after Real lost 4-0 at Liverpool*

Managers are like fish. After a while they start to smell.

Giovanni Trapattoni *on leaving Fiorentina*

There would have to be a bubonic plague for me to pick [Paolo] Di Canio.

Giovanni Trapattoni, *Italy coach*

People say we caught Tottenham at a good time, but we haven't won since Hitler invaded Poland.

Chris Turner, *Peterborough manager, after drawing with Spurs*

When I arrived last summer one of my predecessors told the Spanish press that Meester Terry would be gone by Christmas. He forgot to say which year.

Terry Venables *at Barcelona*

Barca are on a terrible run but I can still go out, as long as it's after midnight, it's a dimly lit restaurant and I'm wearing dark glasses.

Terry Venables

I've told Chancellor Kohl that it's not on for Denmark to want to leave the European Union and, at the same time, be European champions.

Berti Vogts *before his Germany team lost the Euro 92 final to Denmark*

If people saw me walking on water you can be sure someone would say: 'Look at that Vogts, he can't even swim.'

Berti Vogts *on critics of his methods as Germany coach*

Zidane and Vieira? They're only names. I think we can win this game.

Berti Vogts *before Scotland's 5-0 defeat by France in his first game in charge*

Burnley have the potential to be a sleeping giant.
Chris Waddle *on becoming player-manager*

When I'm operating on an ingrowing toenail, I find I'm not listening to my patient. At the end I say: 'I'm sorry, Mrs Kirk, I was away there, picking the team for Saturday.'
Neil Warnock, *then doubling as a chiropodist and Scarborough manager*

It would have taken a brave man not to wear brown pants after looking at Arsenal's team sheet and then at ours.
Neil Warnock *at Notts County*

Tommy Johnson is brainless and talented, which suits our system perfectly.

Neil Warnock *at Notts County*

The closest me and Cloughie have come is when he tried to kiss me after a testimonial match, but I smelled the aftershave and skipped past him.
Neil Warnock *at Notts County*

When I saw Barbra Streisand yell back at a heckler, I thought, At least it's not just me that gets angry at work.
Neil Warnock

For me to get the Manager of the Month award I'd have to win nine games out of eight.
Neil Warnock *at Sheffield United*

I'd love to manage Sheffield Wednesday. I'd buy so many tosspots and f*** 'em up so badly. Then I'd retire to Cornwall and spend my life laughing my f*****g head off.
Neil Warnock *at Sheffield United*

Paddy [Kenny] was in the wrong place at the wrong time. Judging by the photos he was also with someone hungrier than him.
Neil Warnock *after his Sheffield United goalkeeper had an eyebrow bitten off in a restaurant brawl*

I'm known on the internet by my anagram of Colin Wanker. In fact I'm disappointed now if opposing fans don't call me a wanker.
Neil Warnock *at Sheffield United*

I hear Gary [Megson] is writing a book. That's good news for insomniacs everywhere.
Neil Warnock *at Sheffield United*

Mourinho is like a Yorkshireman with a Portuguese accent.
Neil Warnock *at Sheffield United*

I don't get many managers wanting to have a drink with me. There's a few, but I keep their identities quiet in case it damages their reputations.

Neil Warnock

Forest's goals were pure comedy. You could probably win £250 on *Candid Camera* for the second one.

Neil Warnock at Crystal Palace

It's impossible for us to match Chelsea's spending power – unless we find oil at Highbury.

Arsene Wenger at Arsenal

If you look at Arsenal's red cards, it's mostly a case of provocation. Unfortunately it has worked for 52 players.

Arsene Wenger in 2003

We even watched [Cesc] Fabregas in training at Barcelona. How did I do that? With a hat and a moustache.

Arsene Wenger

If they do what they like to do, then we will expose ourselves.

Arsene Wenger

If there is an apology, it must be coming by horseback.

Arsene Wenger after Alex Ferguson alleged that Arsenal 'turned games into battles'

Despite global warming, England is still too cold for him.
Arsene Wenger on José Antonio Reyes' extended loan to a Spanish club

I'm amazed how big Patrick Vieira's elbows are – they can reach players ten yards away.

Arsene Wenger

I gave [Cristiano] Ronaldo a shirt with his name on the back. I'm disappointed that I seduced only his mum.
Arsene Wenger on his unsuccessful wooing of the teenaged Ronaldo

How do you stop Rivaldo? You try to buy him the day before you play him.
Arsene Wenger

He's focused and determined, but also very young. I don't think he even shaves yet.

Arsene Wenger on midfielder Jack Wilshere, 16, after Arsenal beat Sheffield United 6-0 in the Carling Cup

They scored five goals from five breakaways.
Tom Wilkie, St Mirren manager, after losing 5-1 to Falkirk

Cantona gave interviews on art, philosophy and politics. A natural room-mate for David Batty, I thought.
Howard Wilkinson *at Leeds*

If we were getting murdered every week, I'd be panicking. As it is, I'm not anxious.
Danny Wilson, *Sheffield Wednesday manager, before losing 8-0 at Newcastle*

I told my centre-backs that if they can keep their heads while all about them are losing theirs, they're out of position again.
Danny Wilson *at Barnsley*

I'm pleased with the way the girls battled back from a 2-0 defecate.
Rod Wilson, *Lincoln Ladies manager, as quoted in a press release*

I think I've still got a couple of [Roy] Keane's studs in my ankle that I can give back to him.
Gianfranco Zola, *West Ham manager*

3: 'Trousers down': The late, great gaffers

If my players were bricklayers, the house they built would fall down.
Alan Ball *at Portsmouth*

The Old Firm match is the only one in the world where the managers have to calm the interviewers down.
Tommy Burns *at Celtic*

I want to congratulate Scotland for the team they presented to us.
Marcos Calderon, *Peru coach, after beating Ally MacLeod's team in 1978*

If God had meant football to be played in the air, he'd have put grass in the sky.
Brian Clough

If ever I felt off-colour I'd sit next to John Robertson. Compared with this fat, dumpy lad, I was Errol Flynn.

Brian Clough *at Nottingham Forest*

I've got a young team. Acne is a bigger problem than injuries.
Brian Clough *at Forest*

Asa Hartford kept dashing off to mark Mick Mills when we played Ipswich. I got a message out to him saying if he wanted to meet Mills that badly I could arrange an interview after the game.
Brian Clough

Kenny Dalglish wasn't big but where he got his strength from was a huge arse, which came down below his knees.
Brian Clough

I wish Gary McAllister would stop talking about me. I can only assume I upset him when we met because he was wearing cowboy boots and I asked if he was related to John Wayne.
Brian Clough *after McAllister joined Leeds instead of Forest*

Neil Webb isn't actually a very good player, but he's got a lovely smile that brightens my Monday mornings.
Brian Clough

I haven't seen the lad but he comes highly recommended by my greengrocer.
Brian Clough *on signing Nigel Jemson*

I'm not saying Brian Rice is thin and pale, but the maid in our hotel made his bed the other day and didn't realise he was still in it.
Brian Clough

Sheringham was the slowest player in the Forest squad, perhaps due to all those nightclubs he kept telling me he didn't frequent.
Brian Clough

Do you know, Sinatra once met me.
Brian Clough

There are bigger heads than mine in this division. Howard Wilkinson springs to mind.

Brian Clough

Resignations are for prime ministers and those caught with their trousers down, not me.

Brian Clough

My wife says that OBE stands for Old Big 'Ead.

Brian Clough

I'm fed up with Bobby Robson pointing to his grey hair and saying the job has aged him 10 years. If he doesn't like it, why doesn't he go back to his orchard in Suffolk?

Brian Clough

I don't speak foreign languages. I find that 'f*** off' is understood by pretty much anyone.

Brian Clough

The way I deal with unhappy players is that we talk for 20 minutes, then decide that I was right.

Brian Clough

The only person certain of boarding the bus to Wembley for the League Cup final is Albert Kershore, and he'll be driving.

Brian Clough in 1990

I've asked my coach driver to try to knock Gascoigne down if he sees him at Wembley. I don't think we'll stop him otherwise.

Brian Clough *before the 1991 FA Cup final*

Coaching's for kids, not professional players. If a player can't pass or trap the ball, he shouldn't be there in the first place. I told Roy McFarland to get his hair cut. Now that's coaching at the top level.

Brian Clough

I'm as bad a judge of strikers as Walter Winterbottom, who gave me only two caps.

Brian Clough

I'm glad to see Leeds have recovered financially since paying me off a few years ago.

Brian Clough

It's just a walk across the Irish Sea as far as I'm concerned.

Brian Clough *on the possibility of managing the Republic of Ireland*

From now on I'll be taking my holidays in Porthcawl and I've bought a complete set of Harry Secombe albums.

Brian Clough *on his interest in the Wales job*

The River Trent is lovely. I should know because I've walked on it for 18 years.

Brian Clough

As if cutting [Alfie] Haaland in half wasn't bad enough, Roy Keane then swoops over him like Dracula. All he needed was the black cloak.

Brian Clough

I only hit Roy [Keane] the once. He got up, so I couldn't have hit him that hard.

Brian Clough

If the BBC ran a Crap Decision of the Month competition on *Match of the Day*, I'd walk it.

Brian Clough *as Forest faced relegation*

TV REPORTER: Can I have a word from you, Brian?
CLOUGH: Of course. Goodbye.

Brian Clough *after his final match as a manager*

After my heart problem I got a Get Well card which just said: 'I didn't know you had one.'

Brian Clough

To put everyone's mind at rest, I'd like to stress that they didn't give me George Best's old liver.

Brian Clough *after transplant surgery*

Arsenal caress a football the way I dreamed of caressing Marilyn Monroe.
Brian Clough

You can't keep goal with hair like that.
Brian Clough *on David Seaman's ponytail*

I got one or two goals a season, give or take the odd 30.
Brian Clough

They say Rome wasn't built in a day, but I wasn't on that particular job.
Brian Clough

It's no wonder Jim Smith has no hair – he has to start writing the team sheet out on Monday just so he can have all the foreigners' names spelt right by the time Saturday comes around.
Brian Clough

What's his name? Vorti Begts? I don't like Germans. They shot my dad.
Brian Clough *when Berti Vogts became Scotland manager*

I've dropped off to sleep long before Sven-Göran Eriksson has finished droning on. There's more emotion in a dead reindeer.
Brian Clough

They're putting up a statue of me in Derby. The pigeons will be pleased – there will be more room on my head to shit on than anyone else.
Brian Clough

In the 1970s the only agent was 007 and he shagged women, not entire football clubs.
Brian Clough

For all his horses, knighthoods and championships, Fergie hasn't got two of what I've got. And I don't mean balls.
Brian Clough, *two-time European Cup winner with Forest, in 2004*

That José Mourinho's got a lot to say for himself. He reminds me of what I was like at his age – but I was better looking.
Brian Clough

Nigel isn't as bright as me, despite his A levels. And everybody likes him, so there's obviously something wrong.
Brian Clough *on his son as manager of Burton Albion*

There was talk of a stand being named after me. But there was nothing, not even a toilet. They could have had the Brian Clough Bog.
Brian Clough

What am I like at 4.50 on a Saturday afternoon? I'm ill-tempered, rude and wondering what's for tea, same as ever.
Brian Clough *after retiring*

I wouldn't say I was the best manager in the business. But I was in the top one.

Brian Clough

When I go, God's going to have to give up his favourite chair.

Brian Clough

I'm told Blackburn need a big name. Engelbert Humperdinck is a big name but it doesn't mean he can play football.

Ray Harford at Blackburn

You can mark down 25 June 1978 as the day Scottish football conquers the world.

Ally MacLeod, Scotland manager. His team went out in the first round

With a bit of luck in the World Cup I might have been knighted. Now I'll probably be beheaded.

Ally MacLeod

I'd have preferred it if neither England nor West Germany had reached the final in 1966. I'm not a great lover of the Germans – they bombed my folks' house in Clydebank in the war.

Ally MacLeod

All I want you to do, son, is see how fast their No. 9 can limp.
John McGrath, *Port Vale manager, to a centre-half*

I left as I arrived – fired with enthusiasm.
John McGrath *on his sacking by Preston*

I'll listen to offers for all my players, and for the club cat, Benny, who's pissed off because all the mice have died of starvation.
John McGrath *at Halifax*

Things got so bad I received a letter from *Reader's Digest* telling me I hadn't been included in their prize draw.

John McGrath *after his dismissal by Halifax*

Mind you, I've been at Liverpool during the bad times, too. One year we came second.
Bob Paisley

Some of the jargon is frightening. They talk of 'getting round the back' and sound like burglars. They talk about 'positive runs' and being 'too negative', which sounds like you're filling the team with electricians.
Bob Paisley

Jimmy Adamson was crowing after Burnley beat us one year that his players were in a different league. At the end of the season, they were.
Bob Paisley

Well, we scored nine, and you can't do better than that.
Bobby Robson *after England thrashed Luxembourg*

If the pressure had frightened me, I'd have kept my quality of life at Ipswich, driving my Jag six miles to work every day and getting drunk with the chairman every Saturday night.
Bobby Robson *as England manager*

We didn't underestimate Cameroon. They were just a lot better than we thought.

Bobby Robson, *England manager*

What can I say about Peter Shilton? Peter Shilton is Peter Shilton and he has been Peter Shilton since the year dot.
Bobby Robson

On my way to the stadium I followed a car with the number plate SOS1. Perhaps someone was trying to tell me something.
Sir Bobby Robson *on his first day as Newcastle manager*

Titus [Bramble] makes one mistake every game. If he could just correct that bad habit, he'd be one of the best defenders in England.

Sir Bobby Robson *at Newcastle*

On the coach Kieron Dyer suddenly shouted, 'Stop the bus! I've left my earring in the dressing room.' Can you imagine a player telling Bill Shankly: 'Stop the bus, Bill, I've lost an earring.'

Sir Bobby Robson

I was asked which one I'd choose, Viana or Viagra? That's easy. Saturday afternoon, Viana. Saturday night, Viagra.

Sir Bobby Robson *after bringing Hugo Viana to Tyneside*

I'm looking for a goalkeeper with three legs.

Sir Bobby Robson *after Newcastle's Shay Given was 'nutmegged' twice for goals*

I'm not going to look beyond the semi-final, but I'd really love to lead Newcastle out in the final.

Sir Bobby Robson

The trouble with you, son, is that your brains are all in your head.

Bill Shankly *to an unnamed Liverpool player*

I want to build a team that's invincible, so they'll have to send a team from Mars to beat us.
Bill Shankly *at Liverpool*

Brian Clough is worse than the rain in Manchester. At least God stops that occasionally.
Bill Shankly *at Liverpool*

A million wouldn't buy him. And I'm one of them.

Bill Shankly *at Liverpool*

Of course there are two great teams on Merseyside. Liverpool and Liverpool reserves.
Bill Shankly

PRINCESS MARGARET: But Mr Labone, tell me, where is Everton?
BRIAN LABONE: In Liverpool, ma'am.
PRINCESS MARGARET: Of course, we had your first team here last year.
Bill Shankly, *story of the 1966 FA Cup final*

Right, son, nothing clever from you this week.

Bob Shankly, *Dundee manager in the 1960s, to fringe player Craig Brown*

The papers say I'm Celtic's first Protestant manager. I prefer to say 25 per cent of our managers have been Protestant.
Jock Stein *at Celtic*

Rangers are all right, but they still haven't invented blue grass.
Jock Stein *on Celtic's pitch with an English journalist*

If Stan Bowles could pass a betting shop like he can pass a ball, he'd have no worries.
Ernie Tagg, *Crewe Alexandra manager*

I once called English football the working man's ballet. It's more like a clog dance now.
Tony Waddington *at Stoke City*

We've got to focus on the St Johnstone's Paint Trophy game now.
Dennis Wise, *Leeds manager*

4: 'Sheep's testicles': The owners

If, like me, you like a gamble now and again, then what price a flutter on us reaching that top six?

Mike Ashley, *Newcastle owner, in December 2008 – they were relegated in May*

They're building another stand at Villa Park. They're going to call it 'The Other Doug Ellis Stand'.

Ken Bates

I met Steven Gerrard in a London restaurant and offered him the chance to widen his horizons, leave his provincial town and come to Leeds. I said I could only offer a grand a week but he could have all the Yorkshire pudding he could eat.

Ken Bates

Pink is my daughter's favourite colour. She is five. It would've been unthinkable in my day.

Franz Beckenbauer, *Bayern Munich president, on Franck Ribéry's pink boots*

I can't see Mohamed Al Fayed and his entourage of bodyguards and advisers fitting into our gents' toilet at the same time.

Buster Bloodvessel, *Margate chairman and Bad Manners singer, when they drew Fulham in the FA Cup*

I was in talks to open a high-end pizzeria when I got a call about QPR. I was still thinking about food. I thought maybe QPR was a barbecue restaurant.

Flavio Briatore, *Benetton Formula 1 owner, on how he got into football*

I would give Steven Gerrard a contract to shoot a film as he's a very good actor.

Enrique Cerezo, *Atletico Madrid president, after Gerrard won a dubious penalty*

We've got a long-term plan for this club and apart from the results, it's going well.

Ernie Clay, *Fulham chairman*

We're delighted to be competing in Europe. How else can we get our duty-free cigarettes?

John Cobbold, *Ipswich chairman*

What constitutes a crisis at Ipswich? Well, if we ran out of white wine in the boardroom.

Patrick Cobbold, *Ipswich chairman*

Most people who can remember when Notts County were a great club are dead.

Jack Dunnett, *Notts County chairman*

Jo Venglos was always the favourite in the back of my mind.

Doug Ellis, *Aston Villa chairman, springs a managerial surprise*

When [Bosko] Balaban came back after the summer, I said: 'Oh, you're back.' He said: 'You remember me then?' I said: 'With the money I paid for you, I'll never forget you, my son.'

Doug Ellis *on Villa's seldom-seen £6.7m Croat*

The most educated person at Real Madrid is the woman who cleans the toilets.

Joan Gaspart, *Barcelona vice-president*

If Rafa said he wanted to buy Snoop Doggy, we would back him.

George Gillett Jnr, *Liverpool's American co-owner*

Our long-term aim is to make Middlesbrough synonymous with good football rather than chemical plants. We're well on our way, even if Ruud Gullit had never heard of us when we contacted him.

Steve Gibson *in 1995*

Hugo Sanchez is a very dangerous man, as welcome as a piranha fish in a bidet.

Jesus Gil, *Atletico Madrid president, on Real Madrid's Mexican striker*

We'll serve sheep's testicles as a delicacy in the boardroom. There's a lot of sheep in Wales so it's only right they should be represented at Ninian Park.

Sam Hammam, *Cardiff City chairman*

My ambition has long been to lift the FA Cup. Soon I won't be able to hold the bloody thing.

Sir Jack Hayward, *Wolves owner, at the age of 74*

I hope Tony Adams plays because his is the only name I know. All these Viallis, Vieiras and Viagras.

Sir Jack Hayward, *Wolves owner, before a match against Arsenal*

I don't go to the sports pages first. I go to the obituaries, just to make sure I'm not in there.

Sir Jack Hayward

I'm staying on as chairman. No other idiot wants to come forward.

Peter Hill *after Hereford were relegated from the Football League*

Our objective is to keep Arsenal English, but with a lot of foreign players.
Peter Hill-Wood, *chairman*

Real Madrid have turned themselves from a football club into a circus. I've never seen a chimps' tea party like it.
Uli Hoeness, *Bayern Munich director*

The lowest point of the year was hearing that Nick Barmby had used the five worst words in the English language: 'I want to join Liverpool.'
Bill Kenwright, *Everton chairman*

What other job is there where your entire livelihood depends on 11 daft lads?
Francis Lee, *Manchester City chairman, on football management*

We should rename ourselves Coventry Houdini.

Mike McGinnity, *Coventry City chairman*

Tell the Kraut to get his ass up front. We don't pay a million for a guy to hang around in defence.
New York Cosmos *executive on Franz Beckenbauer in the 1970s*

If the *Titanic* had been painted sky blue it would never have sunk.
Bryan Richardson, *Coventry chairman, after another escape from relegation*

Alan Shearer is boring – we call him Mary Poppins.

Freddy Shepherd, *Newcastle director, secretly taped by a tabloid newspaper*

Being chairman of Tottenham was like having diarrhoea.

Sir Alan Sugar

If I fail, I'll stand up, be counted and let some other brain surgeon take over.

Sir Alan Sugar *as Tottenham chairman*

Darren Anderton has had so many X-rays that he got radiation sickness.

Sir Alan Sugar

Americans think that any guy who runs around in shorts kicking a ball rather than catching it has to be a Commie or a fairy.

Clive Toye, *British chief executive of the New York Cosmos*

I received my resignation by email.

Dennis Tueart *on being ousted from the Manchester City board*

5: 'Away with the pharaohs': The commentators

Port Vale have got Gareth Ainsworth playing as a down and out winger.

George Andrews, *local radio commentator*

The Northampton striker went through Stoke's defence like a combine harvester on a summer holiday.

Brian Beard, Sky *reporter*

Batty and Le Saux there, arguing over who has the silliest name.
Rory Bremner *in a spoof commentary after the Blackburn colleagues traded blows*

What a goal by Bergkamp! One for the puritans.
Capital Gold *commentator*

United seem to be in total, if not complete, control.
Jon Champion

Victor Hernandez, like an orchestral conductor directing his troops.
Jon Champion

The full name of this team is Liga Deportiva Universitaria De Quito – a slap in the face for the man who starts the chant 'Give me an L'.
Channel 5 *commentator during the 2008 World Club Cup final*

Poland v England, 7pm tonight, followed by Female Orgasm, 10.50pm tomorrow.
Advert *for Channel 5*

INTERVIEWER: Your eyes are streaming. Are you all right?
CHARLES: Yeah, I'm OK. I've just got clitorises in my eyes.
Mel Charles, *Arsenal player and cataracts sufferer, in a 1960 interview*

Jim Leighton is looking as sharp as a tank.
Barry Davies

The crowd think that Todd handled the ball – they must have seen something nobody else did.
Barry Davies

And the German stormtroopers are arriving at the far post.
Barry Davies

What full-back wouldn't like to have Des Walker inside him?

Peter Drury, radio commentator

BARRY DAVIES: Oh, look at that, between his legs!
DAVID PLEAT: Beautiful, isn't it?
Exchange during Scotland v Morocco coverage

The Preston fans are giving Gerrard abuse but he won't hear it – he's got the blinkers on.
Alan Green

Seaman's jersey seems to have all the colours of the rainbow in it – yellow, red, green, black.
Alan Green

Every man in grey is being booed, particularly the man in yellow.
Alan Green

It was the game that put the Everton ship back on the road.
Alan Green

Shelbourne are obviously having trouble with Bohemians' five-man back four.
Eamonn Gregg, *Irish TV commentator*

Amr Zaki's still away with the pharaohs.
Stuart Hall *on Wigan's absentee Egyptian striker*

And Hyypiä rises like a giraffe to head the ball clear.
George Hamilton, *Irish TV commentator*

Viv Anderson has pissed a fatness test.
John Helm

Martin O'Neill standing hands on hips, stroking his chin.
Mike Ingham

The Uruguayans are wasting no time in making a meal around the referee.
Mike Ingham

The teams are going at it hammer and thongs.
Tony Incenzo *on TalkSport*

Charlton had no team-mate to pass to, so he shot himself.
Hugh Johns

The Republic of Ireland squad will be based in the heart of Tel Aviv in the Holy Land and it's a Mecca for tourists.
Kevin Keatings, *radio reporter*

The Us are playing all in leather. Leather?! I meant yellow.
Neil Kelly *reporting on Colchester on Radio Essex*

He wouldn't say boo to a ghost.
Local radio *commentator at Barrow v Kettering*

Ronaldo can pull anything out of the hat at the drop of a whim.
Paul Masefield, *ESPN Asia commentator*

It looks like a night of disappointment for Scotland, brought to you live by ITV in association with National Power.
Brian Moore

For those of you watching in black and white, Spurs are the team in the yellow.
John Motson

The referee is wearing the same yellow-coloured top as the Slovakian goalkeeper. I'd have thought the UEFA official would have spotted that, but perhaps he's been deafened by the noise of the crowd.
John Motson

Nearly all the Brazilian supporters are wearing yellow shirts. It's a fabulous kaleidoscope of colour.
John Motson

Steve Bruce has got the taste of Wembley in his nostrils.
John Motson

On a scale of one to ten, that was one hell of a strike.
John Motson

I think this could be our best victory over Germany since the war.
John Motson *commentating on England's 5-1 win in Munich*

The ball was glued to his foot, all the way into the back of the net.
Alan Parry, *ITV commentator*

And that's a priceless goal, worth millions of pounds.
Alan Parry

Two-nil is a cricket score in Italian football.
Alan Parry

Hakan Yakin plays with Young Boys in Bern.
Jonathan Pearce

In Norway, the land of the troll, Dennis Wise takes the corner kick.
Jonathan Pearce

It's nil-nil here at Falkirk Stadium. They've been playing here since 2004.
Derek Rae

Brian Deane has gone down like the twin towers, only less spectacularly.
Graham Richards, *Radio Derby commentator, three days after the 9/11 tragedy*

I haven't seen so many grown men hugging and kissing since I watched *Brokeback Mountain* with the missus.
Tom Ross *on BRMB radio, at Aston Villa v Portsmouth*

Aliadière – sadly, more syllables than goals this season.
Setanta *commentator during Newcastle v Middlesbrough*

Derby are being led out by their ram, and not being harsh on Nottingham, but it would be hard for them to be led out by a tree.
Setanta *commentator*

Gazza will literally be going through cold turkey for the rest of his life.

TalkSport *commentator*

Colour-wise, it's oranges v lemons, with the Dutch wearing all white.
Clive Tyldesley

Tuncay really is on his last legs – quite literally.
Clive Tyldesley

It is a penalty decision that could have gone either way – and did!
Clive Tyldesley

Ron, what do you say to a team that's 5-0 up at half-time? I don't suppose you'd know.
Clive Tyldesley to summariser Ron Atkinson

Liverpool have literally come back from the grave!
Clive Tyldesley

Free kick to Preston. Just how fatal will it be to Liverpool?
Clive Tyldesley

England are learning to walk before they can run, with their feet nailed firmly to the ground.
Clive Tyldesley

There's an enormous gulf between the United States and Brazil, and I don't just mean the Gulf of Mexico.
Steve Wilson on USA v Brazil in the Confederations Cup

Ashley Cole is getting a lot of stick, but you'd expect that when you're playing away from home.
Steve Wilson on Portsmouth v Chelsea

Chris Iwelumo's open-goal miss [for Scotland against Norway] was the equivalent of falling out a plane and missing the Earth.
Chick Young

6: 'Rabbit with headlights': The pundits

We've been playing against San Marino for an hour and it has just occurred to me that we're drawing 0-0 with a mountain top.
Ian Archer, *Scottish radio pundit*

Van Nistelrooy chipped it over the keeper. In technical terms, that's what I call a dinky-do.
Jimmy Armfield

This World Cup has got a very international feel about it.
Jimmy Armfield

Chelsea look like they've got a couple more gears in their locker.
Ron Atkinson

Gary Lineker just shook hands with Jürgen Klinsmann. It's a wonder Klinsmann hasn't fallen down.
Ron Atkinson

[Peter] Schmeichel can throw the ball further than I go on holiday.
Ron Atkinson

Someone in the England team will have to grab the ball by the horns.
Ron Atkinson

[Beckham] hasn't got a great technique, technically.
Ron Atkinson

I've had this sneaking feeling throughout the game that it's there to be won.
Ron Atkinson

I'm going to make a prediction – it could go either way.
Ron Atkinson

He sliced the ball when he had it on a plate.
Ron Atkinson

He'll be the most famous Greek for years, even though he's Argentinian.
Ron Atkinson *on Panathinaikos coach Juan Rocha*

There was cool panic from Wes Brown there.
Ron Atkinson

These Iraqis don't take any prisoners.
Ron Atkinson *at the 1986 World Cup, as the Iran–Iraq war raged*

Ian Evatt has gone down easier than my daughter.

Dave Bassett

Blackburn have a few injuries but at least Sandy Rocca Cruz is back.
Dave Bassett

Cudicini is like a rabbit with headlights.
Dave Bassett

An inch or two either side of the post and that would've been a goal.
Dave Bassett

You've got to miss them to score sometimes.
Dave Bassett

The three of them will be acting in tandem.
Peter Beardsley

Throwing food is what children do. We were real men. We'd have chinned them.
George Best *after Arsenal players threw pizza at Sir Alex Ferguson*

[Paul] Gascoigne is accused of being arrogant, unable to cope with the press and a boozer. Sounds like he's got a chance to me.
George Best *when Gazza first emerged*

Gascoigne wears a No. 10 jersey. I thought it was his shirt number but it turns out to be his IQ.
George Best

Most managers would give their right arm for a European Cup, and Bob Paisley had three.
Manish Bhasin, *Football Focus presenter*

If brains were chocolate, Robbie Savage wouldn't have enough to fill a Smartie.

Alan Birchenall

Diouf is a master of the dark art of the winger – he draws you in and then sucks you off.
Garry Birtles

That Kris Commons, he doesn't look much like a footballer. More like an Albanian weightlifter.

Aidy Boothroyd

Our talking point this morning is George Best, his liver transplant and the booze culture in football. Don't forget, the best caller wins a crate of John Smith's.

Alan Brazil

I wouldn't touch Chimbonda with a barn door.

Alan Brazil *on TalkSport*

Sir Alex Ferguson *is* Manchester United. If you cut him he bleeds red.

Alan Brazil

Spurs fans are very boyish about the future.

Alan Brazil

And Roy Keane's face punches the air.

Alan Brazil

Some players need a boot up their backside. Other players need the arm.

Alan Brazil

Let's hope it's not just a case of sore grapes.
Alan Brazil

In their last four Blackburn have lost 3-0, 3-1, 5-3 and 3-2. It doesn't take a rocket scientist to work out that's 12 goals conceded.
Alan Brazil

One moment I'm playing football and the next – whack – I wake up in hospital unconscious.
Alan Brazil

He held his head in his hands as it flashed past the post.
Alan Brazil

The tackles are coming in thick and thin.
Alan Brazil

Villa have had a complete reservation of fortunes.
Alan Brazil on Martin O'Neill's appointment as Aston Villa manager

Villa are making a great challenge to the so-called top four.
Alan Brazil

In a minute I'll be talking to a tremendous left foot.
Alan Brazil

Stoke are fourth in the Championship, and you can't ask for more than that.

Mark Bright

Fraizer Campbell has two great feet, left and right.

Mark Bright

That's football – Northern Ireland have had several chances and not scored, England have had no chances and scored twice.

Trevor Brooking

Martin Keown is up everybody's backside.

Trevor Brooking

They're playing in an Arctic monsoon.

Terry Butcher

And Liverpool's Vegard Heggem, my word, he must have a Honda down his shorts.

Terry Butcher

Albert Riera is looking like the full McCoy.

Steve Claridge

You can't beat everyone up all the time with the same brush.

Steve Claridge

I'm sure Spurs will get another opportunity, hopefully before the final whistle.
Steve Claridge

He's not the brightest tool in the box.
Steve Claridge

If Wenger is still here in ten years and Arsenal haven't won any trophies, will he still be here?
Steve Claridge

Martin Jol was literally a dead man walking at Spurs.
Steve Claridge

Three into five just won't go.
Steve Claridge

Unfortunately they just haven't had their shooting or heading boots on today – or whatever you wear on your head when you head the ball.
Steve Claridge

Lady Luck tried his best for Liverpool there.
Steve Claridge

Tottenham are conceding more goals than you would expect them to, and they're letting them in at the other end.
Ray Clemence

If he can find a ground where he scored a league goal, I'll meet him there.
Brian Clough *on a dispute with fellow TV pundit Jimmy Hill*

Trevor Brooking floats like a butterfly and stings like one too.
Brian Clough

Robbie Keane was like the cat that got the cheese.
Stan Collymore

It's going to take time for Tony Adams to inflict his style on Portsmouth.

Stan Collymore

This sums up the ridiculum of the situation.
Stan Collymore

I'm not saying [Andy] van der Meyde is a bad winger. He just can't cross the ball.
Johan Cruyff

I used to love playing against English teams. They always gave you the ball back if you lost it. Still do.

Johan Cruyff

James Beattie isn't as young as he used to be.

Jason Cundy

Aston Villa are breathing down their throats.

Kenny Cunningham

Scotland will be home before the postcards.

Tommy Docherty *on the 1998 World Cup. They did well to get a point*

Usually all teams get at Millwall is the tyres let down on their coach.

Tommy Docherty

If that lad makes a First Division footballer, my name is Mao Tse Tung.

Tommy Docherty *on Dwight Yorke in 1991*

Jimmy Hill is to football what King Herod was to baby-sitting.

Tommy Docherty

The only time Ray Wilkins gets forward is to toss the coin.

Tommy Docherty

Paul Scholes is literally on another planet.
Kieron Dyer

The Arsenal youth team is full of young players.
Robbie Earle

Senegal will be kicking themselves because they've shot themselves in the foot.

Efan Ekoku

INTERVIEWER: Soccer Saturday – it's radio on TV, isn't it?
JEFF STELLING: You don't see any shots at goal. You don't see any goals. You don't see any real action. It's just like watching West Brom.
Exchange in an online interview with the Sky anchor

JEFF STELLING: Spurs–Portsmouth. Anyone gone close, Chris?
CHRIS KAMARA: No. But there have been a few near misses.
Exchange on Sky

DAVID PLEAT: Here comes the surging Brazilian right-back. He's Argentinian, actually.
CLIVE TYLDSLEY: He's Uruguayan.
Exchange on ITV

HUGH JOHNS: Well, Sir Alf, when do you think we might get the floodlights back on?
SIR ALF RAMSEY (SUMMARISER): I am not an electrician.
Exchange on ITV when the lights failed during the 1974 World Cup

PAUL GASCOIGNE: I've never heard of Senegal before.
DES LYNAM: I think you'll find they've been part of Africa for some time.
Exchange on ITV, 2002 World Cup

RICHARD KEYS: Is there anything you've learnt about Robbie [Fowler] from working with him?
RIO FERDINAND: Well, if you see his ears close up, they're quite small.
Exchange on Sky

CONOR MACNAMARA: And that was a wayward shot by Valencia.
MARK LAWRENSON: Almost ended up in Valencia.
Exchange on Radio 5 Live at Wigan v Spurs

GARY LINEKER: Trevor Brooking is in the Sapporo Bowl. What's it like, Trevor?
TREVOR BROOKING: Well, it's a bowl shape, Gary.
Exchange during BBC coverage of the 2002 World Cup

GARY LINEKER: Do you think Rio Ferdinand is a natural defender?
DAVID O'LEARY: I think he could grow into one.
Exchange on BBC TV, 2002 World Cup

In the Scottish Cup you only get one crack at the cherry against Rangers or Celtic.

Tom Ferrie

Anyone can beat anyone else in this league and to prove this there were seven draws yesterday.

Don Goodman

The chief scout and manager must be in unicism with each other.

Bobby Gould

I've sat on the hot seat and felt its hotness.

Bobby Gould

The keeper was like a rabbit in the headlines.

Bobby Gould

The good people of Suffolk will be looking forward to this one.

Bobby Gould *on Norwich v Bayern Munich*

Just look at the results that Steve McClaren hasn't produced.

Bobby Gould

Anyone who takes drugs should be hammered.
Andy Gray

There are a lot of tired legs wearing Tottenham shirts.
Andy Gray

He [Roque Santa Cruz] doesn't look a million per cent happy.
Andy Gray

I was only saying the other day how often the most vulnerable area for goalies is between their legs.
Andy Gray

If the Black Death ever swept through London again I wouldn't even want to be in the next street to Darren Anderton, because you can be sure he'd get it.
Jimmy Greaves

I settle down to watch every England game [under Eriksson] at 8pm. An hour and a half later my watch says 8.15.
Jimmy Greaves

Gazza is capable of breaking both leg and wind simultaneously.

Jimmy Greaves

Davie Hay will still have a fresh pair of legs up his sleeve.
John Greig

Pink is a woman's colour, or so my missus tells me.
Ron 'Chopper' Harris *on Arsenal striker Nicklas Bendtner's pink boots*

Last year's Scottish title race was a bit of a damp squid.
Mark Hateley

Carroll needed a composed finish there, but he took a wild slash at it.

Craig Hignett

I understand Eto'o, Henry and Messi have 90-odd goals between them this season. I'm not surprised, but it is surprising.
Glenn Hoddle

If it doesn't go right tonight, Wenger has got another leg up his sleeve.
Glenn Hoddle *on a two-leg Carling Cup semi-final*

I thought [Joey] Barton's bum cheeks looked very pert. Nice and tight, no cellulite.
Ian Holloway *after Barton bared his backside*

If we're talking lookalikes, Avram Grant's Toad of Toad Hall, isn't he?

Ian Holloway

If the ball were a woman she'd be spending the night with [Dimitar] Berbatov.

Ian Holloway

Give Beckham a knighthood? You're having a laugh. He's just a good footballer with a famous bird.

Ian Holloway

He's six foot something, fit as a flea, good-looking – he's got to have something wrong with him. Hopefully he's hung like a hamster. That would make us all feel better. Having said that, me missus has got a pet hamster at home, and his cock's massive.

Ian Holloway on Cristiano Ronaldo

Look at the state of Neil Warnock. His head was coming off and quite rightly so.

Ian Holloway

Liverpool have played with no real convention.
Ray Houghton

I've been playing in a golf day for a boy seriously injured in a car accident. I had to drive like a lunatic to get here.
Ray Houghton *on why he was late on-air on TalkSport*

Trevor Francis couldn't spot a great footballer if the bloke's name had four letters, started with 'P' and ended with 'e'.
Alan Hudson

They call Gerard Houllier the French professor. I can only say I'm glad he wasn't the professor who operated on me when I was rattling the pearly gates.
Alan Hudson *doubting Houllier's wisdom in buying Emile Heskey*

To get £80m is an offer you can't refuse to turn down.

Paul Ince *on Cristiano Ronaldo's transfer*

If they [modern-day players] aren't happy, they throw their prams out and want to leave straightaway.
Paul Ince

I've got four words for you: Coppell for QPR. Hang on, that's not right. I'll check it... six words.
Ronnie Irani

Coming up, we'll speak to Coventry chairman Ray Ranson at the Rioja Arena.
Ronnie Irani

The tension is palatable.
Matt Jackson *at Hull v Stoke*

That's the 64 dollar question.
Leighton James, *TV pundit and ex-Wales winger*

Isn't that always the way sometimes?
Paul Jewell

Peter Crouch's handball was so blatant you could see it on the radio.
Gary Johnson

You have to say Stoke are defending like beavers.
Chris Kamara

Even Stevie Wonder would have spotted that handball.
Chris Kamara

Jesus Christ, if I start losing sleep over Phil Babb I'm in trouble.
Roy Keane *on his former team-mate turned Sky pundit*

I wouldn't trust some of these people to walk my dog.

Roy Keane *on the TV pundits when he was Sunderland manager*

There's only one team that's going to win now and that's England. I hope I'm not tempting providence there.

Kevin Keegan *on ITV, seconds before Romania's winner at France 98*

Gary always weighed up his options, especially when he had no choice.

Kevin Keegan

Sunderland have edged this one by a long, long way for me.

Kevin Keegan

Sky gets its money from prescription payers.

Martin Keown

See ya. Daft little ground, silly game, f*** off.

Richard Keys, *Sky presenter, unaware he was on air as pictures of the Faroe Islands v Scotland came on*

[Italy defender] Apolloni doesn't know whether it's New Year or New York.

Mark Lawrenson

Portugal play everything through the middle – they've got less width than Bernard Manning.

Mark Lawrenson

Most players would give their right arm for Jason Wilcox's left foot.
Mark Lawrenson

Martin O'Neill looks like a man who's got nits and worms at the same time.
Mark Lawrenson *on the Aston Villa manager's frantic touchline style*

Portugal have had more possession but less of the ball.
Mark Lawrenson

He's like 6ft 4in of blancmange, more Swiss Toni than Luca Toni.
Mark Lawrenson

England are being numerically outnumbered in midfield.
Mark Lawrenson

Michael Owen isn't the tallest of lads but his height more than makes up for that.
Mark Lawrenson

They're in pole position, i.e. in third position, for the Champions League.
Mark Lawrenson

It was like the Sea of Galilee – the two defenders just parted.
Mark Lawrenson

You need at least eight or nine players in a ten-man wall.
Mark Lawrenson

Fulham have been slowly sinking to the bottom very, very quickly.
Mark Lawrenson

I'm not saying he's going to field a weakened team. It just won't be as strong.
Mark Lawrenson

There's no argument, Nicolas Anelka is arguably in the form of his life.
Mark Lawrenson

Arsenal have been written off so often you can't write them off.
Matt Le Tissier

There's nothing more horrible than some big galoot coming up your backside with no protection.
Matt Le Tissier

Had [Martin] Taylor not broken Eduardo's leg with that tackle we'd have said 'that's a leg-breaking tackle'.
Matt Le Tissier

Apart from setting up the second goal and having a hand in the third, Emmanuel Adebayor didn't really do anything.
Matt Le Tissier

I know medicals are definitely a lot more thorough than they were in the past. And I don't even know what they were like in the past.
Matt Le Tissier

The World Cup is every four years so it's going to be a perennial problem.
Gary Lineker

The best way to watch Wimbledon is on Ceefax.

Gary Lineker on the 'Crazy Gang'

Even Poirot would struggle to find evidence that Brugge are a good side.

Gary Lineker

So Portsmouth have won the FA Cup. I don't want to alarm you, but the last time that happened World War Two broke out.
Gary Lineker

There's Eastlands in the distance, Manchester City's ground. Or should I say Middle-Eastlands.

David 'Bumble' Lloyd, *cricket pundit, at a Test match at Old Trafford*

Fourteen million of you were watching the [England] game on ITV – that's 87 per cent of the population.

Gabby Logan

That was actually only a yard away from being an inch-perfect pass.

Murdo MacLeod

Steve McManaman once described Zinedine Zidane as ridiculous. You can't get a higher compliment than that.

Jason McAteer

None of the Celtic players stood up and counted.

Frank McAvennie

Joaquín scuffed that shot with his chocolate leg.

Mick McCarthy

I can't say England are shite because they beat us in the Euro 2000 play-offs, and that would make us even shittier.

Ally McCoist

Where is the Americans' defence? It's like the back four of the *Marie Celeste*.
Ally McCoist *during Iran v USA*

Arsenal and Spurs? No chance. The two best clubs in London are still Stringfellows and the Hippodrome.
Terry McDermott, *ex-Liverpool player, in 1988–89, when Arsenal won the Championship*

It looks as if Hearts have reverted to a five-man back four.
Alan McInally

Chimbonda was good for that one season at Wigan. Now he moans more than my ex-wife.
Alan McInally

When it comes to the David Beckhams of this world, Ian Harte's up there with Roberto Carlos.
Duncan McKenzie

Theo Walcott is a little bit invisible.
Steve McManaman

Owen Coyle has worked a miracle at Burnley, because let's face it, it's only a village.

Billy McNeill

Some of Spurs' best players are illegible for the UEFA Cup.
Gary Mabbutt

Comparing Gascoigne with Pelé is like comparing Rolf Harris to Rembrandt.
Rodney Marsh *after the 1990 World Cup*

Peter Schmeichel is working as a BBC pundit, but you could put a parking meter next to Alan Hansen and I'd find it more interesting to watch it click round.
Rodney Marsh

Berbatov can see things with the outside of his boot.
Alvin Martin

Brian Laws has lifted his team out of precocious waters.
Alvin Martin

Van der Vaart isn't renowned for his trademark headers.
Brian Marwood

It's very pedestrianised.
Andy May, *Radio Manchester summariser, on Schalke v Manchester City*

I'd play Viduka all day long, even if it's only for 45 minutes.

Paul Merson

Ronaldo did about nine leg-overs there.
Paul Merson

Boulahrouz likes to get right up your backside and make you turn the other way.
Paul Merson

Three million for a player is hardly anything. I had three million once.
Paul Merson

That free kick was so wide it nearly hit my car.
Paul Merson

Liverpool were all mishy-mashy. I know that's not a word, but it should be.
Paul Merson

Middlesbrough keep flirting with relegation and if you keep walking past the barbers, eventually you'll get a haircut.
Paul Merson

Boro have lost games they should have won, and that's down to inexperience and not having enough experience.
Paul Merson

Ian Ashbee is very underrated and it's right that he gets all the accolades he gets.
Paul Merson

[Robin] Van Persie is the right player for Arsenal – he can open a can of worms.
Paul Merson

Too many of the England players looked like fish on trees.
Paul Merson

I fear for Hull now. They are the downfall of their own loss.
Danny Mills

City aren't used to playing two-legged football.
Danny Mills on Manchester City in the UEFA Cup

The Danish people love Stig Tøfting's no-nonsense style. With him there's no flicks and farts.
Jan Molby

Spurs have now got what I would call an English manager.
Alan Mullery on Harry Redknapp

There's only one team looking like scoring here. Scunthorpe have had all the play. Burnley look very tired. Hang on – Burnley have scored.

Alan Mullery

Nikos the Greek [Burnley goalkeeper Nikolaos Michopoulos] is getting his hands on everything. Except that one – one-all.

Alan Mullery *at the same game*

James McFadden has been a taliban for Scotland.

Charlie Nicholas

I'm not sure George Burley is any closer to solving his solution.

Charlie Nicholas

I've no idea what Arsene Wenger paid for him. It was four million plus.

Charlie Nicholas

Lee Hendrie is Lee Hendrie and he always will be.

David O'Leary

Ireland don't have the players they used to – the O'Learys, the Stapletons, the Bradys.

David O'Leary

Pavel Nedved's deceptively quick, even when he's completely stationary.
Russell Osman

Celtic were once nine points ahead, but somewhere along the road their ship went off the rails.
Richard Park

Peter Crouch is absolutely centrifugal to Sven's plans.
Mike Parry

How important will the goalkeeper be for Arsenal tonight?
Ian Payne, Sky presenter, before a penalty shoot-out with Roma

The Pope may be Polish, but God is a Brazilian.
Pelé after Brazil beat Poland in the World Cup

In the cold light of day you go to bed at night thinking about the chances you've missed.
David Platt

Andorra will literally park the bus in front of goal.
David Pleat

For such a small man Maradona gets great elevation on his balls.
David Pleat

Chelsea are wearing the white of Real Madrid and that's like a red rag to a bull for Barcelona.
David Pleat

Steve Claridge is as silly as Mr Simple and as happy as Larry.
David Pleat

It looked a little bit worse than it appeared.
David Pleat

Sometimes football turns on the slightest biscuit of good fortune.
David Pleat

Cristiano Ronaldo has been compared with George Best, the incomparable George Best.
David Pleat

Germany benefitted there from a hand-job on the goal-line.
David Pleat *after Germany's Torsten Frings handled*

The ball is in play a lot of the time, which is good to see.
David Pleat

For Arsenal, the sight is in end.
David Pleat

They're going to bring on a couple of substitutes, probably from the bench.
David Pleat

We've been unindated with text messages.
Mick Quinn

When I think of Sheffield Wednesday, the first name that comes to mind is always Lee Hurst. Sorry, David Hirst.
Mick Quinn

After that goal you could literally see Arsenal's players deflating.
Mick Quinn

He's nearly decapitated his head off.
Mick Quinn

There's only a limited number of places in the top six.
Mick Quinn

Steven Gerrard makes runs into the box better than anyone. So does Frank Lampard.
Jamie Redknapp

He'll be like a father figure to him.
Jamie Redknapp on Peter Schmeichel and his goalkeeping son Kasper

That's Arsenal – they're either brilliant or inconsistent.
Jamie Redknapp

The ball literally explodes off his foot.
Jamie Redknapp *on Ronaldo's 40-yard strike against Porto*

I don't know what state of mind his body's in.
Jamie Redknapp *on Stoke's Ricardo Fuller*

There will be a game when someone scores more than Brazil, and that may just be the game they lose.
Sir Bobby Robson

I'd say he was the best in Europe, if you put me on the fence.
Sir Bobby Robson

You have to, you know, to some degree, er, admire the Germans.
Sir Bobby Robson *on the 2002 World Cup finalists*

The Tartan Army can be our tenth man tomorrow.
Alan Rough *before Holland v Scotland*

When Jason Koumas is on form, he's the type of player who calls all the strings.

Ian Rush

He's already on a yellow card, so now he's really treading the boards.
John Salako

No one has more legs than Park and no one has more lungs than Rooney.
John Salako

Solskjaer hit that with his unpopular left foot.
Lawrie Sanchez

The whole transformation of the game has just turned.
Teddy Sheringham

Get your players on who can unlock the door and sooner or later they will break the door down.
Tim Sherwood

Ravanelli, Juninho... Bryan Robson has certainly brought some big names to Middlesbrough. But it's like going to a club and getting off with a big blonde. The lads will say: 'Phwoar!' But can you keep her?
Bernie Slaven

Pepe Reina must be tearing his hair out.
Graeme Souness *after Liverpool lost to Lyon*

Great striking partnerships come in pairs.
Nigel Spackman

Rafa Benitez will be keeping at least two eyes on the Champions League.
DJ Spoony *on Radio 5 Live*

And a goal for Sheffield Wednesday by Guylain Ndumbu-Nsungu. Local boy makes good.
Jeff Stelling

David Goodwillie got that goal, so it's probably a good thing that I've got to press on.
Jeff Stelling

They'll be dancing in the streets of Total Network Solutions.
Jeff Stelling *after victories by the Welsh club*

Fernando Torres is a certain starter. Is he starting, Alan?
Jeff Stelling

I didn't see the Eduardo incident so I've no idea how bad it was but it was obviously absolutely horrendous.
Jeff Stelling

Gareth Jelleyman of Mansfield Town has been sent off. Hope he doesn't throw a wobbly.
Jeff Stelling

Macclesfield are going back to basics – they've signed Reid and Wright.
Jeff Stelling

They've got the game by the throat in the neck.
Trevor Steven

Agbonlahor is not quick. But he's fast, very fast.
Graham Taylor

If it stays as it is, I can't see it altering.
Graham Taylor

Very few of us have any idea whatsoever what life is like living in a goldfish bowl, except of course those of us who are goldfish.
Graham Taylor

We can all see that when Djibril Cissé opens his legs he's very hard to handle.

Graham Taylor

Chelsea have no width, and they're not playing in what I like to call the corners of the pitch.
Graham Taylor

A Thai chairman with a Swedish manager. It could only happen at Manchester City.

Graham Taylor

Reading's six-foot-two lads are five foot eleven this year.

Phil Thompson

If the Liverpool board are going to wash their dirty linen in public they should do it behind closed doors.

Phil Thompson

Worse than the overpaid boys in shorts are the overpaid commentators in long trousers. They have 'analysis' where they watch bits over again in a manner that suggests short-term memory loss may be an issue. One replay showed a man falling over for no apparent reason. 'Did you see him fall over?' asked the pundit, making one question his assessment of the average level of viewer intelligence.

Sandi Toksvig, broadcaster and writer

'What did you think of the winners?' asked the man in charge. 'They were organised,' declared the expert, making one long for disorganised football where people run on to the pitch willy-nilly using their own ball.

Sandi Toksvig

Billy Davies will need every tool in the book today.
Andy Townsend

Ljungberg desperately wants to suck in Cocu.
Andy Townsend

Jan Koller was literally, literally up his backside there.
Andy Townsend

My head was literally spinning.
Andy Townsend

Fernando Torres's English seems to be coming on good.
Andy Townsend

Scotland can't afford to take their minds off the gas.
Andy Townsend

The Dutch have tasted both sides of the coin now.
Andy Townsend

The Belgians will play like their fellow Scandinavians, Denmark and Sweden.

Andy Townsend

You could have driven a Midnight Express through that Turkish defence.

Terry Venables

You would think if anyone could put up a decent wall it would be China.

Terry Venables *after Brazil scored a free kick*

Like so many of the Chelsea team, Zola is unique.

Barry Venison

They've got to concentrate on the way they've concentrated.

Barry Venison

Let Gerrard go forward and say to Barry: 'You anchor.'

Chris Waddle

Arsenal's touch and movement are amazing. I hope the listeners are watching this.

Chris Waddle *on Radio 5 Live*

The one thing Ronaldo has is pace, quick feet and a great eye for goal.
Chris Waddle

One thing Robbie Keane will give you – work rate, guile, skill and effort.
Paul Walsh

Alan Shearer has banged it through a gap that wasn't even there.
Paul Walsh

It looks like no one at the BBC is ever going to tell Alan Shearer that 'he has went' is not English.
When Saturday Comes *magazine*

Being a Uruguayan, Paolo Montero is obviously a nasty character.
Ray Wilkins

In any walk of life, if you put quality balls into the box you're going to cause problems.
Ray Wilkins

Pretty soon they'll all be going out on the pitch with satellite dishes stuck up their arses.
Ian Wright *on the pervasive influence of TV*

The ref was booking anyone – I thought he was filling in his Lottery numbers.
Ian Wright

7: 'Still in the toaster': The comics and celebrities

The France team all tested positive for being assholes.
***Lance Armstrong**, former Tour de France winner, after France lost to Italy in the 2006 World Cup*

Those nuts. Running around in shorts, chasing a big ball like a bunch of schoolkids.
***Joe Azcue**, Cleveland Indians baseball coach*

When Bruce Rioch became Millwall manager we were depressed and miserable, but he has turned it all round. Now we're miserable and depressed.
Danny Baker, *Millwall fan and broadcaster*

I respect Gazza. He goes up to journalists and says 'F*** off!'
Danny Baker

Rumour had it Julian Dicks picked up the No. 23 shirt when he joined Liverpool because it said Fowler on it.
Kevin Baldwin, *author, on the much-booked defender*

Vinnie admits throwing toast at Gary Lineker. What he doesn't say is that it was still in the toaster.
Tony Banks MP

God gave Gazza enormous footballing talent but took his brain out to even things up.
Tony Banks MP

If there was a footballers' special on *The Crystal Maze*, featuring the England team, their task would be to try to order pizza.
Frankie Boyle, *Scottish comedian, lampoons footballers' intelligence on Mock the Week*

How can you lie back and think of England
When you don't even know who's in the team?
Billy Bragg *song lyric*

It's weird 'You'll Never Walk Alone' being a football anthem because it comes from an old musical. I'd like to go down to Millwall and hear them singing 'How Do You Solve A Problem Like Maria?'

Jo Brand

I remember when I had to tell my dad I wasn't going to become a footballer. I said, 'Dad, I'm doing a performing arts degree.' He said, 'Why are you doing this to me?' I said, 'I don't know. Maybe I can show you through expressive dance.'

Alan Carr, *gay comedian and son of ex-Northampton manager and player Graham Carr*

David Icke says he's here to save the world. Well, he saved bugger all when he played in goal for Coventry.

Jasper Carrott

I hear Glenn Hoddle found God. That must have been one hell of a pass.

Jasper Carrott

My programme has been switched to accommodate David Beckham and his boyfriends chasing an inflated sheep's pancreas around some field in Portugal.

Jeremy Clarkson, *Top Gear presenter*

Ally McCoist is handsome, rich, funny and happy. My envy knows no bounds.
Billy Connolly

This staunch Stoke fan is getting earache from his missus. 'You'd rather go and watch Stoke City than take me out.' 'Correction,' he replies. 'I'd rather go and watch Port Vale than take you out.'
Pete Conway, *Potteries comedian*

Q: What's the difference between Jesus and David James?
A: Jesus saves.
Elwin Crockett, *West Ham club chaplain*

White Hart Lane is a great place. Only one thing wrong with it – the seats face the pitch.

Les Dawson

Sigmund Freud once said humour was as incongruous as a buckled wheel, but he never played the old Glasgow Empire on a wet Monday night after Rangers and Celtic had both lost on Saturday.
Ken Dodd

MRS MERTON: Is it your ambition to play in a World Cup final?
VINNIE JONES: I play for Wales.
Exchange *on TV's Mrs Merton Show*

The England team are a bag of shite. My gran would do better on acid with a Toblerone stuck up her arse.
Liam Gallagher *of Oasis in 2000*

I'm extremely grateful to Gazza and all he has done because at least people are going to spell my surname properly.
Bamber Gascoigne

So this movie you star in, *The Life Story of George Best*. Tell us what it's about.
George Gavin, *TV presenter, to Best*

All I want for Christmas is a Dukla Prague away strip.

Half Man Half Biscuit *song title… about Subbuteo*

The trouble with Mohamed Al Fayed is that he doesn't understand British traditions and institutions. I mean, he took over Fulham and made them successful.
Andy Hamilton

Football is a pantomime of pain and disappointment.
Nick Hancock *on supporting Stoke City*

Peter Beardsley is the only player who, when he's on TV, the Daleks hide behind the sofa.
Nick Hancock

Shearer is so dull he once made the papers for having a one-in-the-bed romp.

Nick Hancock

When a manager rests players because they have played two games in six days, I laugh my cock off.

Ricky Hatton, *boxer and Manchester City fan*

If we'd had rugby union's ten-metre rule in our game, Willie Miller of Aberdeen would have played most of his football in Norway.

Tony Higgins, *Scottish players' union official*

I saw a Newcastle season ticket nailed to a tree. I thought, I'm having that. Well, you can never have enough nails, can you?

Matthew Horne

Manchester United? I don't know them. How much are they?

Michael Jackson

All this talk about Tommy Docherty not being fit to run a football club is rubbish. That's exactly what he's fit for.

Clive James

In English football, if you've got two GCSEs you get called Prof.

Boris Johnson

For those of you watching in black and white, Liverpool are the team with the ball.

Joke *on Merseyside during Liverpool's dominance under Bob Paisley*

Q: Why is Nayim the most virile player in Europe?
A: Because he can lob Seaman from 50 yards.

Joke *by Tottenham fans after Arsenal lost the 1995 Cup-Winners' Cup final*

People ask me how hard Tommy Smith was when he played for Liverpool. All I can say is he was born on 5 April 1945 and a few weeks later Germany surrendered.

Steve Kindon, *after-dinner speaker and former Burnley and Wolves striker*

The US finally came up with an exit strategy. Unfortunately it's for the World Cup.

Jay Leno *in 2006, three years after the US-led invasion of Iraq*

I once spent ages in a bar talking to a chap I thought was the pop singer Seal. I later found out he was someone called Ruud Gullit.

Laurence Llewelyn-Bowen

I'm not trying to take over Portsmouth. I don't even know where it is. All I know is that a lot of sailors live there.

Frank Maloney, *boxing promoter*

Have we got any Man United fans in the audience? Course we have – we're in Hammersmith. Every gig I do there's a United fan. They're like rats – you're only ever three metres away from one of the b*******.

Jason Manford

This male MP was found dead in stockings and suspenders. He was also wearing a Manchester City scarf but police kept that bit quiet so as not to embarrass the relatives.

Bernard Manning

How can anyone call Ginola lazy? He's a sex symbol and has all that hair to blow-dry every day. That's an hour's job in itself.

Simon Mayo, *Radio 5 Live presenter*

Q: What do you think of Manchester United?
A: They're cheating, whingeing scumbags.

Rory McGrath, *comedian and Arsenal fan*

Keane has said he'll stay with United through thick and thin, or Becks and Posh as they're known.

Rory McGrath

If Gazza farts in front of the Queen, we get blemished.

Paul McGaughey, *Adidas spokesman, on the risks of a sponsorship deal*

Georgie Best, you were a sixties sensation, weren't you? You know all that marvellous football you played and then of course all the booze – did you ever think if you hadn't done all that running around playing football, would you have been as thirsty?
Mrs Merton

I sent my son to one of Bobby Charlton's schools of excellence and he came back bald.
Mrs Merton

Soccer will never take over from baseball. Baseball is the only chance we blacks get to wave a bat at a white man without starting a riot.

Eddie Murphy

Germaine Greer said that Cheryl Cole isn't a feminist, as a healthy girl is a fat-bottomed creature. What nonsense. Cheryl does have a big arse – he's called Ashley.
Al Murray hosting Have I Got News For You

If there's anything to moan about, Gary [Neville] will find it. He's worse than Victor Meldrew.
Tracey Neville, netball-international sister of the England defender

Corpus Christi, Oxford, have beaten Manchester United in the final of *University Challenge*.
Newsreader *on Radio 4 in 2009, when Manchester University were beaten finalists*

It's just as well he's not allowed to head the black in.
John Parrott, *snooker professional, on playing son-in-law Duncan Ferguson*

Scorer for Kilmarnock, number 16, Dick Turpin.
Public address announcer *at Motherwell alleging robbery after a last-minute winner against his team*

Jeff [Astle] had this window-and-office cleaning business. His slogan was: 'We never miss a corner.'

Frank Skinner *after the death of his West Brom hero*

I was going to ask him about my idea for an El Tel-themed nightclub called Wormwood Scribes, but I chickened out.
Frank Skinner *on meeting Terry Venables, following legal problems over his Scribes West club*

I was watching Germany on TV and got up to make a cup of tea. I brushed against the telly and Klinsmann fell over.
Frank Skinner

Rooney has signed a deal to do five books. That's an awful lot of crayons.

Johnnie Walker, *Radio 2 DJ*

Posh Spice is pregnant. At least that's one time David Beckham has stayed on long enough.

Bradley Walsh *after Beckham was sent off in the 1998 World Cup*

At the League Cup final this guy behind me was yelling: 'Savage, you cheating, long-haired gypsy Welsh c***.' I had to turn to him and say: 'Oi, mate, less of the Welsh.'

Paul Whitehouse, *comic actor and Welsh Tottenham fan*

What you call football is like cricket to us Americans.

Andy Williams, *singer*

I love it when Gazza smells the referee's armpits and he can't do anything about it.

Franco Zeffirelli, *Italian film director*

8: 'See Naples and Dai': The press

If you ever predict my team right, I'll give you a free weekend up in Loch Lomond. And I'll make sure the midges are out for you.
Sir Alex Ferguson to the press

You lot had me out of the door three years ago. You had me in a bath-chair down on Torquay beach.
Sir Alex Ferguson to journalists in 2009

You've enthralled me all season with your honesty, integrity – and nonsense!
Sir Alex Ferguson. One reporter replied: 'Likewise'

Let people get *The Beano* or *The Dandy*, or some Agatha Christie novels. There's plenty of reading material out there, Jesus Christ!
Sir Alex Ferguson *when reporters told him people wanted to read about Wayne Rooney*

I love you all – I've come to spread peace!
Sir Alex Ferguson *to the media before winning the 2008 Champions League final*

Now, if you could just let us have your names and the newspapers you work for, we'll know who to ban.
Ken Bates *at his first Leeds press conference*

You are not my friend, you are a journalist. If you invited me to dinner then I would not attend.

José Mourinho

JOSÉ MOURINHO: Maybe you should pick the team.
REPORTER: If you gave me part of the nine million euros you earn, I would.
MOURINHO: It's not nine, it's 11, and with sponsors it comes to 14.
Exchange *at an Inter Milan press conference*

I know the media all love me. They must care about me because they're always asking me if I'm going to stay or go.
Avram Grant *before his last match as Chelsea manager, the Champions League final v Manchester United*

You people are like those serial killers you see in films who cut out letters to make up things like 'Your wife is next'.
Gordon Strachan *to the press at Celtic*

The press in Barcelona are always there – they want to come home and sleep with you.
Thierry Henry

No comment, gentlemen. You just make it up anyway.
Steve Coppell *to waiting reporters*

You're all such nice people. Sometimes I wonder who writes all the articles.
Sven-Göran Eriksson *to journalists covering England*

The English press are a very nice bunch of bastards.
Graham Taylor, *England manager*

I used to quite like turnips. Now my wife won't serve them.
Graham Taylor *after the Sun branded him a turnip*

I'm beginning to wonder what the national vegetable of Norway is.
Graham Taylor, *England manager, after being compared with a turnip and onion after games v Sweden and Spain*

I've told the players never to believe what I say about them in the papers.
Graham Taylor *at Aston Villa*

I don't kick dressing-room doors, or the cat, or even journalists.
Arsene Wenger

You guys probably write the truth. Then in the office the editors chop out the important things. Like facts.
Kevin Keegan *to the press at Newcastle*

No, I won't tell you my team. Hitler didn't tell us he was sending over those doodlebugs, did he?
Bobby Robson *to the press*

It's nice to be stabbed in the front for a change.

Terry Venables *on the Australian media*

I'm off to my 300-acre farm. You lot can bugger off to your council houses.
Ken Bates *to the press after Chelsea were relegated*

REPORTER: Martin, have you made any New Year resolutions?
MARTIN O'NEILL: Yes I have – and most of them involve you.
Exchange *at an Aston Villa press conference*

I've always said there's a place for the tabloid press in football. They just haven't dug it yet.

Tommy Docherty

Football journalists? They're just about able to do joined-up writing.

Sir Alan Sugar

Never say never, and never believe a newspaper.

Bora Milutinovic, *Serbian coach*

The press in England make from a little mosquito a big elephant.

Ruud Gullit *at Chelsea*

The papers reckoned we played badly last week, when I thought we were fantastic. Shows how much I know.

David O'Leary, *Leeds manager*

As it was the media who tipped us to win, I thought one or two of their jobs might be in jeopardy. Not likely – it was me they were after.

Bobby Robson *recalls England's failure at Euro 88*

Players get upset when old pros criticise them in the papers. They just think: What an old git.

Alan Smith, *Daily Telegraph writer and ex-Arsenal and England striker*

You lot got rid of Neil Kinnock. You must be able to do something about referees.

Bobby Gould, *Coventry manager, to a press conference*

What the f***'s a rhetorical question?
Steve Bruce *to a reporter who said he wanted to ask one*

Strictly off the record, no comment.
Colin Murphy, *Lincoln manager*

I don't trust anyone that doesn't have self-doubt. But I'm walking tall right now. I've got a lot of faith in myself and my team. It feels like the right thing to do. Is this too deep for the *Daily Mail*?
Tony Adams *at Portsmouth*

Dear monkeys, Look in the mirror. You are one step away from becoming human beings. Your leader Mowgli is greedy and makes you collect rotten stories from cesspits and poison readers with them. This is unworthy even of monkeys.
Vladimir Romanov, *Hearts chairman, in an open letter to the press*

You shouldn't be training your lenses on our bedroom windows. The French people don't care whether Fabien Barthez sleeps in underpants or boxer shorts.
Willy Sagnol, *France defender, to photographers at the 2006 World Cup*

They were Rotherham fellas, writing in a Rotherham paper for other Rotherham fellas, so bugger impartiality.
Bill Grundy, *TV presenter, on his early career as a football reporter*

SCOTTISH REPORTER: Welcome to Scotland, Sir Alf.
ALF RAMSEY: You must be f*****g joking.
Exchange at Prestwick Airport after England arrived to play the Scots, 1968

I cover Everton matches too, but if war was declared I think I know which side I'd be on.
Tommy Smith, *ex-Liverpool player, on his media work*

We're on the march with Allah's Army.
Headline in the Scottish Sun *before Morocco v Scotland*

Zidane appears and leaves Beckham in his underwear.

Headline in Spain's Marca *newspaper after the France captain's two late goals beat England*

Becks Dumps Posh!
Headline on Leeds United website after Jermaine Beckford scored two against Peterborough

Frog on the Tyne
Headline in the Daily Star *after David Ginola joined Newcastle*

The wally with the brolly

Headline in the Daily Mail *on Steve McClaren's rain-lashed swansong as England manager*

Baddy long legs

Headline in the Sun *after Peter Crouch was sent off*

Queen in brawl at Palace

Headline in the Guardian *from 1970, when Crystal Palace had a striker called Gerry Queen*

Norse manure!

Headline in the Scottish Sun *after Norway 0 Scotland 0*

Super Caley Go Ballistic, Celtic Are Atrocious

Headline in the Scottish Sun *after Inverness Caledonian Thistle won at Celtic*

Swedes 2 Turnips 1

Headline in the Sun *after England lost to Sweden at Euro 92*

Swede 1 Beetroot 0

Headline in The Times *after Sven-Göran Eriksson beat Sir Alex Ferguson in the Manchester derby*

Krankies 0 Krankl 2

Headline in the Daily Record *after Scotland lost to Hans Krankl's Austria*

This is Anfield – so what?
Headline in Marca *newspaper the day before Liverpool beat Real Madrid 4-0*

I turned Ronaldo on with my Tesco knickers – exclusive.

Headline in the News of the World *alleging prostitute romps with the Manchester United star*

Our football is like our inflation: 100 per cent.
Headline in Brazilian paper after victory over England in 1981

Germany – the mega blancmange!
Headline after the Germans' disastrous Euro 2000

Not only the cows are mad in England. The English press are also infected.
El Mundo Deportivo *newspaper after Spain-bashing stories during Euro 96*

Some shocking graffiti outside Goodison Park. Look how they've left the 't' off 'Rooney must diet'.
Steve Anglesey, Daily Mirror *columnist*

Former England captain Alan Shearer will manage Newcastle United for the remainder of the season... Shearer will stand in for Roy Kinnear, who is recovering from heart surgery.
Reuters *agency report*

David Unsworth's swerving shot beat the despairing dive of Derby keeper Patriot Fellatio.

Report *in the* News of the World *with Patrick Filotti's name corrupted by a computer spell-check.*

The ridiculous English eat sausages and eggs for breakfast, drive on the left, play baseball with an oar, set times for drinking and think they are the best.

Article *in Portuguese newspaper* 24 Horas *before Portugal v England, Euro 2004*

He had 18 years as a player with Framham and West Bromwitch, was manager for Ibswich and for England after the 1982 World Cup when Mr Wood Green retired.

Egyptian Gazette *on Bobby Robson*

Ten modern labours of Hercules: 1 Make Kenny Dalglish laugh uncontrollably.

Journo-lists *section,* Mail on Sunday *magazine*

The Quakers are likely to be without Greg Blundell tomorrow as the striker struggles with a dead calf.

Report *on Darlington in the* Northern Echo

The word in Italy is 'see Naples and Dai'.

Desmond Hackett *in the* Daily Express *when Welsh minnows Bangor City played Napoli in the European Cup-Winners' Cup*

How football has changed. Now clubs are booking the cooks.
Henry Winter in the Daily Telegraph *after Delia Smith bought into Norwich City*

Alex Ferguson refusing to speak to MUTV is like Joseph Stalin blanking Pravda.

David Lacey, Guardian

David Batty would probably get himself booked playing Handel's 'Largo'.
David Lacey, Guardian

Mr Martinez, the referee, was slow to realise that the Dutch invented the clog.
David Lacey in the Guardian *on the rough side of Holland*

They'll probably call it the Matthews funeral.
Matthew Engel, Guardian *sports writer, after the death of Stan Mortensen, who scored a hat-trick in the 'Matthews final'*

Billingham Synthonia is the only club named after a fertiliser, although several other candidates spring immediately to mind.
Harry Pearson, Guardian

If Ossie Ardiles had gone to Arsenal instead of Spurs, they would have had him marking the opposing goalkeeper.
Danny Blanchflower, Sunday Express

People talk about Newcastle being a sleeping giant, but they make Rip van Winkle look like a catnapper.

Hugh McIlvanney, The Sunday Times

As a vision of the future, Graham Taylor's intention [to get England playing a more direct style] ranks right up there alongside the SDP and the Sinclair C5.

Joe Lovejoy, Independent

Sheffield Eagles [rugby league team] play the ball on the ground more than Sheffield United.

Jonathan Foster, Independent

I kept wondering which team had soiled their underpants more with the fear of making a mistake.

Paul Breitner, *former West Germany captain, in* Bild *newspaper*

We're talking about a man capable of going three rounds with a urinal.

Richard Littlejohn *on Paul Gascoigne*, Daily Mail

Nobody cares whether or not Graeme Le Saux is gay. What makes him the most reviled man in football is the fact that he reads the *Guardian*.

Piers Morgan, Daily Mirror

His problem was that they kept passing to his wrong feet.
Len Shackleton, *ex-England player and* People *columnist*

Newcastle have been unlucky with injuries. The players keep recovering.
Len Shackleton

I've heard of players selling dummies, but Newcastle keep buying them.
Len Shackleton

Middlesbrough signing Fabrizio Ravanelli is like someone buying a Ferrari without having a garage.
Giancarlo Galavotti, La Gazzetta dello Sport

Biathlon. Luge. Soccer. Three of a kind.
Cleveland Plain Dealer *newspaper on the US staging the 1994 World Cup*

They're going to bring this thing to the US in '94 and charge people money to watch it? If this thing were a Broadway show, it would have closed after one night.
Frank Depford *in US paper* The National *after the 1990 World Cup final*

In soccer, 21 guys stand around and one does a tap dance with the ball.

Jim Murray, *American sportswriter in the 1960s*

The most exciting moment came when Taddy Smith's powerful drive sailed out of the ground and straight through the window of a nearby house.
Report *in the* Whitby Gazette

Since Hartlepool last scored you could have watched all three *Godfather* movies, waded through every technicolor moment of *Gone With the Wind*, and still had time to settle down to a two-hour episode of *Inspector Morse*.
Editorial *in the* Hartlepool Mail *on the club's record-breaking goalless run*

Secret pictures, gained by our intrepid Albion reporters, have unearthed Stoke's secrets. They train with cannons, rescued from local medieval ruins. Footballs are loaded into them and fired into the distance for Sidibe to head and Fuller to chase.
Report *on Stoke's victory over West Bromwich Albion in the Albion programme in 2007*

My story last week about Fabio Capello was illustrated with a picture, not of the new England manager but of Irish builder Michael McElinney, a professional Capello lookalike. Apologies to Mr Capello and congratulations to Mr McElinney – a remarkably small number of readers spotted the difference.
Correction *in the* Evening Standard's Homes & Property *supplement*

In last week's feature on the history of Southampton FC we inadvertently credited the club's president, Ted Bates, with the role of the poet laureate, Ted Hughes.
Apology *in Southampton's* Daily Echo

Commodore already sponsors Tessa Sanderson, Chelsea FC and a football team, Bayern Munich.

Computer Guardian

Harry Redknapp lookalike requires cash for corrective surgery to avoid Bagpuss jibes.

Advert in Private Eye *magazine*

RON SAUNDERS: Giving the press boys the usual old rubbish, Ron?
RON ATKINSON: Yes, Ron. I was just telling them what a good manager you are.

Exchange after a match in the 1980s

REPORTER: What's the John Gidman situation, Ron? Is he in plaster?
RON ATKINSON: No, he's in Marbella.

Exchange after a Manchester United match

REPORTER: You've got a mountain to climb in the second leg, haven't you?
STEWART HOUSTON: There are no mountains in Wolverhampton.

Exchange after QPR lost at home to Wolves in the League Cup

REPORTER: Do you have a Churchillian speech up your sleeve for games like this?

PAUL JEWELL: I'll just say what I usually say: 'Get out there and win the f*****g game, you c****!'

Exchange in press briefing before a vital Wigan match

REPORTER: What will you do if you win the World Cup?

ALLY MACLEOD: Retain it.

Exchange before Scotland's ill-fated 1978 World Cup campaign

REPORTER: Did you realise it's Wales' worst home defeat in 98 years?

JOHN TOSHACK: I didn't, but I've broken records all my life, so that's another one.

Interview with the Wales manager after a 5-1 loss to Slovakia

BRAZILIAN REPORTER: What do you think of Brazil?

KENNY DALGLISH: I think he's a great player.

Exchange at a press conference during the World Cup finals, 1982. Alan Brazil was in the Scotland squad

REPORTER: You looked tense tonight, Mick.

MICK MCCARTHY: You want to try sitting in the dugout when it's your arse in the bacon slicer.

Exchange after the Republic of Ireland played Saudi Arabia in the 2002 World Cup

REPORTER: Gordon, you must be delighted with that result.

GORDON STRACHAN: Spot on. You can read me like a book.

Exchange after a Southampton victory

REPORTER: What was your impression of Leeds?

STRACHAN: I don't do impressions.

Exchange after a draw at Strachan's old club

REPORTER: What area did you think Middlesbrough were superior in?

STRACHAN: That big grassy one out there for a start.

Exchange after a defeat

REPORTER: Do you think you're the right man to turn things round?

STRACHAN: No. I was asked if I thought I was the right man and I said, 'No, they should have got George Graham because I'm useless.'

Exchange on Strachan's unveiling as Southampton manager

REPORTER: Bang goes your unbeaten run. Can you take it?

STRACHAN: No. I'm just going to crumble like a wreck. I'll go home, become an alcoholic and maybe jump off a bridge.

Excange after a Southampton defeat

REPORTER: Is Klinsmann Spurs' biggest-ever signing?

OSSIE ARDILES: No. I was.

Exchange at a press conference after Ardiles bought Klinsmann

REPORTER: Were you concerned when a bottle was thrown on?

JIM MAGILTON: Listen, I grew up in Belfast – do you think I'm going to be worried about one bottle?

Exchange at the Ipswich manager's press conference

REPORTER: Have you ever used public transport?
GEORGE WEAH: Yes. I've been in a taxi.
Newspaper interview with the former Chelsea striker

REPORTER: What would you have done if you hadn't been a footballer?
CHRIS SUTTON: A funeral director. I like looking at dead bodies.
Exchange from a Chelsea magazine interview

REPORTER: Is your surname a help or a hindrance?
PAUL DALGLISH: I don't know. I haven't had any other name.
Newspaper interview with Kenny Dalglish's son

REPORTER: Why did you take Jack Wilshere off?
ARSENE WENGER: It was 9.25, past his bedtime.
Exchange after Wilshere, 16, played for Arsenal

REPORTER: Are you worried about Chernobyl?
JOHN TOSHACK: Who's he – left-back for Dinamo?
Exchange before Kiev v Real Madrid match

REPORTER: It was a funny game, Jim.
JIMMY SIRREL (NOTTS COUNTY MANAGER): Human beings are funny people.
Exchange at a post-match press conference

REPORTER: How do you stop Thierry Henry?
EDDIE GRAY (LEEDS MANAGER): Punch him and knock him out.
Exchange after Arsenal beat Leeds 5-0

REPORTER: Does it suit you to be the underdogs?

BORA MILUTINOVIC: I must tell you I do not like for me or my players to be called dogs.

Interview with the Serbian coach to the USA

REPORTER: Do you remember where you were when United won the Treble in '99?

DENIS IRWIN: Oh yes. I was playing left-back.

Exchange in Nuts magazine

REPORTER: What's the worst insult you've had from a crowd?

ROBBIE SAVAGE: 'Robbie Savage takes it up the a***' I guess. And I hear 'gyppo' a lot because I suppose I look like a tramp. But the worst thing that's ever been said was someone comparing me to an Afghan hound. That upsets you.

Interview in FHM magazine

ROBINHO: Chelsea made me a great proposal and I accepted.

REPORTER: You mean Manchester City, right?

ROBINHO: Yeah, Manchester. Sorry!

Exchange at the press conference to unveil City's £32.5m Brazilian

What do you mean there's two Manchester teams?

Caption on picture of Robinho circulated on the internet

George Burley will be at the Urban Brasserie, not the Urban Brassiere as previously advised.
Rob Shorthouse, *Scottish FA press officer*

Slim Jim Baxter had everything required of a great Scottish footballer. Outrageously skilled, totally irresponsible, supremely arrogant and thick as mince.
Alastair MacSporran, The Absolute Game *fanzine*

There haven't been so many headbands and leather necklaces since the Allman Brothers played on *The Old Grey Whistle Test*.
When Saturday Comes *magazine on the 'hairy' Argentinians*

Liberia are the worst team to feature a European Footballer of the Year since George Best turned out for Dunstable Town.
When Saturday Comes *on George Weah's international woes*

9: 'Available for panto': The referees

There's a saying in football – 'You'll never see a racehorse refereeing a match'.
Graham Poll

My dad used to referee me when I was a kid. I remember him booking me – and asking my name.
Kevin Kyle, *Coventry striker*

My wife told me that the entire row in front of her stood up to give me the V-sign. I asked what she did and she said she didn't want them to know who she was so she stood up and joined in.
Neil Midgley *on his debut as a top-flight referee*

At Stoke once an elderly lady was waiting for me by the dressing room after the game. She said: 'Mr Knight, I'd just like to say I'm 74, and a grandmother, and you're the worst f*****g referee I've ever seen.' Certainly put me in my place.
Barry Knight

The radio link will be a great help once we get used to it, but I'm still not sure where to put my microphone.
Steve Dunn, *referee*

I know where the linesman should've stuck his flag – and he'd have had plenty of help.
Ron Atkinson *at Coventry*

Referees are like wives. Once you accept that they're always right, your life gets a lot better.
Gary Speed, *Bolton midfielder*

The referees say they are human and I have to believe them on that.

Andy Gray

I've seen harder tackles in the half-time queue for meat pies than the ones punished in games.
George Fulston, *Falkirk chairman*

Then my eyesight started to go and I took up refereeing.

Neil Midgley

I have nothing against the visually handicapped as such. I'm just surprised they are allowed to referee at this level.

The Soup, *Kidderminster Harriers fanzine*

If we're going to have sponsored referees, maybe we could approach Optrex or the Royal National Institute for the Blind.

Paul Durkin, *Premiership referee*

I said to him [Graham Poll]: 'I didn't know you were a Tottenham supporter.' He took exception.

Graeme Souness, *sent-off Blackburn manager*

The ref [Jeff Winter] was a big-time homer, more interested in his rub-on suntan.

David Moyes, *Everton manager*

Anyone who craps in Graham Poll's toilet can't be all bad.

Jeff Winter *after Robbie Savage admitted using Poll's dressing-room loo*

Urs cheated on me and it sounds like he has cheated on England.

Franziska Meier, *former wife of Urs Meier after the Swiss referee disallowed a goal for England*

I've no qualms about playing in one of Uriah's charity golf events, though I may be tempted to wrap my five-iron around his neck.

Dave Jones, *Wolves manager, on Uriah Rennie's 'diabolical' refereeing*

Sir Alex Ferguson once complimented me on my handling of a game. Three weeks later, after I'd refereed another United match, he pulled me aside and said: 'Well, Jeff, back to normal. F*****g business as usual.'

Jeff Winter

If the ref [Andy D'Urso] had stood still we wouldn't have had to chase him.

Roy Keane

In the tunnel I say to David Elleray: 'You might as well book me now and get it over with.' He takes it pretty well but still books me.

Roy Keane

I do like Crystal Palace's ground. There's a Sainsbury's next to Selhurst Park so it's a chance to get some of the weekend shopping out of the way.

David Elleray, *referee*

I can't understand why the ref wasn't more sympathetic. After all, we used to go to the same bookies.

Steve Claridge, *Portsmouth player-manager*

That linesman is as dangerous as a monkey with two pistols.
Gregorio Manzano, *Real Mallorca coach*

A film called *Passport to Terror* will follow and I think this referee will be in it.
Desmond Lynam *on a card-happy Syrian referee*

The referee was bobbins. If you need that translating, it means crap.
Dave Jones, *Southampton manager*

We've got the drug testers here today. I assume they'll ignore the players and go straight to the referee and his assistants.
Mick McCarthy *after a controversial defeat for Wolves*

Usually I like to get kissed before I get screwed.

Mick McCarthy *after the same match*

For that ref to give us a penalty we would have had to pick his pockets, nick his clothes and take his boots.
Mick McCarthy

These days you only have to fart in the box to concede a penalty.

Kevin Blackwell

I understand [Everton manager] Walter Smith described the referee as diabolical. I didn't think he was as good as that.
Jim Smith, *Derby manager*

This referee is so poor that I'd have got booked just getting off the bus.
Norman Hunter

The lad was sent off for foul and abusive language but he swears blind he didn't say a word.

Joe Royle *after Oldham's Paul Warhurst was sent off*

It takes some believing for a referee to mix up two players as different – I'm 5ft 8in and white, he's 6ft 4in and black.
Tony Spearing, *Plymouth defender, after he was booked in mistake for Tony Witter*

I never comment on referees and I'm not going to break the habit of a lifetime for that prat.
Ron Atkinson *after West Brom lost to Red Star Belgrade*

Referees should be wired up to a couple of electrodes. They should be allowed three mistakes – then you run 50,000 volts through their genitals.
John Gregory *at Aston Villa*

Can anybody tell me why they give referees a watch? It's certainly not for keeping the time.
Alex Ferguson

The referee is available for Christmas pantomime or cabaret.
Keith Valle, Bristol Rovers PA announcer, thinking the microphone was switched off

He got the penalty decision all wrong. But he got the minute's silence before the game right.

John Gregory, Aston Villa manager

The ref was a disgrace though he did get three things right – the kick-off, half-time and full-time.
Andy Ritchie, Oldham manager

I thanked the referee for giving us three cracking throw-ins, even when one of them might have been their ball.
Neil Warnock, Notts County manager

Thank God the referee and his linesmen are all out there together. Otherwise they could have ruined three matches instead of one.
Tommy Docherty

We had a Mauritian referee against Paraguay. Mauritius is a lovely island, but they don't play football.
Evaristo Maceda, Iraq coach at the World Cup finals

This is what happens when you have village referees at the World Cup.

Christian Vieri *after England's Graham Poll disallowed two 'goals' for Italy*

We were unlucky to run into a referee who ought to be thinking more about his diet than his refereeing.

Alessandro Nesta *blaming an Ecuadorian official for Italy's World Cup defeat by South Korea*

When a player says 'shit' as he trips over the ball, it doesn't usually mean he has slipped on a dog poop.

Bishop of Haslingden, *a former referee*

I'm back refereeing in the Argentine League and receiving as much shit as ever.

Horacio Elizondo, *2006 World Cup final referee*

I saw someone eyeing me in the pub. I asked: 'Do I know you?' He said: 'You should. You sent me off today.'

Sonya Home, *referee*

In our article 'Off: The rise and rapid fall of Britain's flashiest referee', we used a photograph of Mark Clattenburg and Helen Henderson whom we described as his fiancée. The photograph was taken in 2000 and Helen Hattenburg is no longer Mr Clattenburg's fiancée but his former wife.

Correction in Independent

Our report implied that a player who scored two goals was given an advantage because he was the referee's son. This was incorrect and the goals were scored without the help of the referee.

Apology in the Ilkeston Advertiser

10: 'Show us Uras': The fans

One song, we've only got one Song.
Liverpool *fans' song when Rigobert Song played for them*

He's fast, he's red, he talks like Father Ted, Robbie Keane.
Liverpool *song on their Irish striker*

He's big, he's red, his feet stick out the bed, Peter Crouch.
Liverpool *homage to the towering forward*

Can we play you every week?
Havant & Waterlooville *fans as they led 1-0 at Liverpool*

We all live in a Robbie Fowler house.
Song *by various fans after reports of Fowler's extensive property portfolio*

He's cracking up, he's cracking up, he's cracking, Rafa's cracking up!
Manchester United *fans' song to the tune of 'Three Lions'*

City's going down with a billion in the bank.
Manchester United *fans as their Arab-financed neighbours struggled in 2009*

Forest's going down with a fiver in the bank.
Derby *fans*

You're just a shit Chas and Dave.
Tottenham *fans' song to Liam and Noel Gallagher*

You're just a fat Maradona.
Stoke City *to Carlos Tevez*

Cedric, Cedric, show us Uras.
Falkirk *fans to French defender Cedric Uras*

You can stick your flat-pack wardrobes up your a****.
Northern Ireland *fans at a match against Sweden*

You should have stayed on the telly.
Liverpool *fans to temporary Newcastle manager Alan Shearer*

I predict a Fryatt, I predict a Fryatt.
Leicester *homage to Matty Fryatt to a Kaiser Chiefs song*

You may be Posh, but you're not Royals.
Reading *fans to their Peterborough counterparts*

He's fat, he's round, he swears like Chubby Brown, Joe Kinnear, Joe Kinnear.

Newcastle *fans on the club's interim boss*

When the ball hits your head
And you're sat in Row Z
That's Zamora.
Fulham *song as Bobby Zamora's goal drought continued*

Agadoo, doo, doo, push pineapple shake the tree
Agadoo, doo, doo, football in a library.
Hull City *supporters at Chelsea*

Sell your tower and build a ground.
Barnsley *fans to Blackpool at half-finished Bloomfield Road*

Here for the shot-putt, we're only here for the shot-putt.
Leeds *fans while trailing Rotherham 4-1 at Don Valley Athletics Stadium*

Randy, Randy, buy 'em a roof.
Aston Villa *fans to chairman Randy Lerner on the uncovered away end at Gillingham*

Juan Pablo Angel, there's only Juan Pablo Angel.
Aston Villa *fans*

You don't know what you're doing.
Leeds *fans as a Derby fan proposed to his girlfriend on the pitch at half-time*

You *do* know what you're doing.
Cardiff *fans after the referee disallowed a goal for Coventry*

Is there a fire drill, is there a fire drill?
Arsenal *fans to fellow supporters leaving the Emirates Stadium early*

Deep-fry yer pizzas, we're gonna deep-fry yer pizzas.
Scotland *fans in Italy*

Deep-fry yer long boats, we're gonna deep-fry your long boats.
Scotland *fans in Norway*

Deep-fry yer vodka, we're gonna deep-fry yer vodka.
Rangers *fans to their Zenit St Petersburg counterparts*

Sing when you're whaling, you only sing when you're whaling.
Adelaide United *fans' song against Kashima Antlers of Japan*

What's it like to stink of fish?
Millwall *fans to Grimsby supporters.*

You stole my holiday.
Newcastle *fans at West Ham, whose sponsors, holiday company XL, had gone bust.*

Are you Woolworths in disguise?
Hibernian *fans' song to supporters of cash-strapped rivals Hearts*

John Carew, Carew. He likes a lap-dance or two. He might even pay for you. John Carew, Carew.
Aston Villa *fans after their striker was caught visiting a gentlemen's club*

Bexhill, it's just like watching Bexhill.
Brighton *fans' song during a defeat at Southend*

Oh when the Saints go Johnstone's Paints, Oh when the Saints go Johnstone's Paints.

Bournemouth *fans' song on news of Southampton's relegation to the third tier*

Bees up, Luton down.
Brentford *fans' song to the tune of 'Knees Up Mother Brown' as they celebrated promotion and Luton were relegated*

Leighton Baines, I bet you think this song is about you.
Everton *fans to the tune of Carly Simon's 'You're So Vain'*

He's got a bird's nest on his head
West Ham *fans to Everton's big-haired Marouane Fellaini*

Who needs Robinho, we've got Delap's throw.
Stoke City *fans' song at Manchester City*

You should've gone Christmas shopping.
Reading *fans' song when their team led 4-0 at Bristol City*

You're not special any more.
Manchester United *fans to José Mourinho after knocking Inter Milan out of the Champions League*

That coat's from Matalan.
Manchester City *fans' song to the overcoat-wearing Mourinho*

Who needs Mourinho, we've got our physio.

Scunthorpe *fans' song after physio Nigel Adkins became manager and won promotion*

Get your mascot off the pitch.
AFC Hornchurch *fans to Peterborough's diminutive Dean Keates*

David James superstar
Drops more bollocks than Grobbelaar.
Manchester United *fans' song*

Burn your Ferraris, we're gonna burn your Ferraris.
Real Madrid *fans' song after a 5-1 loss to Zaragoza*

Made out of Lego, your ground is made out of Lego.
Fulham *fans' song at Chester's Deva Stadium*

Stand from Ikea, you got your stand from Ikea.

Millwall *fans' song at Leyton Orient*

You are our feeder club.
Tottenham *fans' song to West Ham supporters*

That's why you're going down.
Reply *by West Ham fans*

5-1, even Heskey scored.
England *fans in Germany in 2006 recalling victory five years earlier*

You're Camp and you know you are.
Ipswich *fans to QPR goalkeeper Lee Camp*

Strawberry blond, yer havin' a laugh.
QPR *fans to Crystal Palace's ginger-haired Ben Watson*

Does your butler know you're here?
West Ham *fans' song to supposedly 'posh' visiting Fulham supporters*

Does your livestock know you're here?
Colchester *fans' song to their Norwich counterparts*

He's tall, he's black, he's had a heart attack, Kanu, Kanu.
Arsenal *fans' song*

He's tall, he's quick, his name's a porno flick, Emmanuel, Emmanuel.

Arsenal *fans' song in praise of Petit*

Are you Tamworth in disguise?
Burton Albion *fans to Manchester United in the goalless FA Cup tie*

Are you Wigan in disguise?
Bolton *fans' song at Bayern Munich*

Let's pretend we've scored a goal.
Derby *fans' song in 6-0 defeat by Aston Villa. They then burst out cheering*

You're just a town full of rugby.
Manchester United *fans' song at Hull City*

Next year, you'll be City fans.
Manchester City *fans' song as their newly wealthy club played Chelsea*

Live round the corner, you only live round the corner.
Chelsea *fans to the 'Cockney' supporters of Manchester United*

We all agree, Asda is better than Harrods.
Charlton fans at Fayed-owned Fulham

We all agree, *Emmerdale* is better than *Brookside*.
Halifax fans' song during an FA Cup tie at Merseyside club Marine

Come on a skateboard, you must've come on a skateboard.
Nottingham Forest fans to Yeading's 60 followers at their FA Cup tie

You're just a fat Eddie Murphy.
Newcastle fans to Jimmy Floyd Hasselbaink

He's short, he's fat, he's gonnae get the sack, Advocaat.
Scotland fans after a 1-0 win over Dick Advocaat's Holland team

He's fat, he's round, he's taken Leicester down.
Reading fans' taunt to former manager Mark McGhee

Armani's number one.
The Kop after David James began modelling

He's tall, he's skinny, he's going to Barlinnie.
Celtic fans when ex-Ranger Duncan Ferguson was jailed

We all agree, *Tiswas* is better than *Swapshop*.
The Kop during a dull period in a Liverpool match in 1980

Peter Shilton, Peter Shilton, does your missus know you're here?
North Bank Highbury *to the England goalkeeper after allegations of his marital infidelity*

We all agree, Des Walker's worth more than Derby.
Nottingham Forest *fans' song*

Steve Foster, Steve Foster
What a difference you have made.
Manchester United *fans when Foster played for Brighton in the 1983 FA Cup final replay, won 4-0 by United, after being suspended for the first, drawn game*

It's not much fun when 50,000 are singing 'Posh Spice takes it up the ****' every weekend.

Victoria Beckham

The fans want to sing, and unless you're Val Doonican you can't do that sitting down.
Kevin Keegan *on all-seated stadiums*

We'll race you back to London.
Arsenal *fans' chant to home supporters at Old Trafford*

Come and have a go if you think you're hard enough.
Manchester City *fans' chant as new world welterweight champion Ricky Hatton took his seat*

You're going home in a military ambulance.
Swindon *fans' chant during a strike by ambulance personnel*

I'm going home in a St John ambulance!
Bolton *chant at Sheffield United as a female St John nurse walked past*

Dicks out! Dicks out!
Fulham *chant when Alan Dicks was manager*

Man-in-a-raincoat's blue-and-white army.
Tottenham *chant. They did not want to use ex-Arsenal manager George Graham's name*

Hyde! Hyde! What's the score?
Preston *fanzine title recalling North End's 26-0 win in 1887*

Sing When We're Fishing.

Grimsby Town *fanzine*

Who's your next messiah – Ant or Dec?
Aston Villa *fans' banner as Newcastle slid to relegation*

Make sure the Sky cameras don't catch you snivelling into your scarf or blubbering into your best mate's shoulder.
Newcastle's *official website urges fans to 'show dignity' before the game that sent them down*

Well done Mary Poppins.
Sunderland *fans' banner 'congratulating' Alan Shearer as Newcastle went down*

The missus thinks I'm working
And I've lied to the gaffer
Cos I'm here in Istanbul
With Stevie G and Rafa
Liverpool banner in Istanbul at the Champions League final

For those watching in blue and white, this is what the European Cup looks like.

Liverpool banner at a Champions League semi-final against Chelsea

José Mourinho: Special One My Arse!
Liverpool banner

Ronaldinho – Our Cilla wants her teeth back.
Slogan on a banner at Liverpool v Barcelona game

U messed up Vietnam. U messed up Iraq. Don't mess with Scousers by giving Rafa the sack.
Poster held on The Kop against Liverpool's American owners

Owned by Americans. Managed by a Spaniard. Watched by Norwegians.
Everton banner at the derby with Liverpool

Manchester 08 – European Capital of Trophies.
Banner at Old Trafford mocking 'European Capital of Culture' Liverpool

United, Kids, Wife – In That Order.
Manchester United *fans' banner*

Shame Carlsberg don't do boards of directors.

Southampton *fans' banner*

Superman wears Tim Cahill pyjamas.
Everton *banner*

Jimmy Abdul. One man, one goal, 36,000 hotel cancellations.
Millwall *banner at Wembley play-off final. Leeds fans had reportedly booked hotels for the final before Abdul scored to knock them out*

You are more ugly than Camilla.
Juventus *supporters' banner message to their Liverpool counterparts*

We'll be in Seville. You'll be watching *The Bill*.
Celtic *banner before the UEFA Cup final in Spain, aimed at Rangers fans*

Jesus is a Wiganner.
Wigan Athletic *banner after Jesus Seba signed from Zaragoza*

Paul McGrath limps on water.
Derby *fans' banner*

Mel's Marvels 5 Fergie's Wallet 1.
Manchester City *banner after the derby triumph by Mel Machin's team in 1989*

Communism v Alcoholism.
Tartan Army *banner at Soviet Union v Scotland match*

Anneka Rice – A Challenge: Get a Drink in Genoa.
Scotland *fans' banner during the 'dry' World Cup of 1990*

Kendall robbed Derek and Mavis.
Manchester City *banner when Howard Kendall rejoined Everton at the time of a mystery theft in Coronation Street*

Forget Ulrika – There's only one Good Johnsen.
Chelsea *banner to Eidur Gudjohnsen*

Mama! Get the pasta on!
Italy *fans' banner as Denmark and Sweden drew to eliminate the Italians from Euro 2004*

We won't need Viagra to stay up.
Charlton *banner before they were relegated in 1999*

Devonshire's the cream, Rice is the pudding.
West Ham *banner at the 1980 FA Cup final v Arsenal, when Alan Devonshire faced Pat Rice*

Maggie Thatcher isn't the only one with Crooks at No. 11.
Tottenham *banner at the civic reception after Garth Crooks helped them win the FA Cup in 1981*

We've come to get our bicycles back.

Holland *fans' banner at a match against West Germany. The Germans had confiscated the Dutch people's bikes during World War II*

We had Sol but he's not a soldier.

Notts County *banner after Sol Campbell's one-match stay at the club*

Jack, are the Villa really more important than our marriage? It's over, Jess.

Banner *draped over a bridge near Villa Park*

To John Hutley from your wife! Happy 30th wedding anniversary for today. Enjoy the match because you're going to pay for it later! Love, Jane

Message *on Millwall's electronic scoreboard*

What will you do when Christ comes to lead us again?
Move St John to inside-right.

Sign and graffito *outside a Liverpool church*

2004 Premiership.
2005 Championship.
2007 Sinkingship.
2008 Abandonship.

T-shirt slogan *as Leeds slipped into the third tier of English football*

1976 was a strange year for English football – Manchester City won a trophy.
T-shirt slogan *on stalls outside Old Trafford.*

We love Robben – just like the Scousers.
Chelsea *fan's T-shirt slogan at Liverpool*

The Silence of the Rams.
Slogan *on an anti-Derby T-shirt sold outside Nottingham Forest*

Sex, beer, football. Have I forgotten something?
Denmark *fans' T-shirt slogan at Euro 2004*

Dear God, Thankyou for Birds, Booze, Fags and Football. Ave It.
T-shirt slogan *in 2009*

I'd rather have Bruce Grobbelaar trying to throw a game than Dave Beasant trying to win one.
Southampton *fan on a radio phone-in*

Would the owner of a blue Opel Corsa near the main entrance please attend to it. You have left your sunroof open and the birds may relieve themselves on your seats.
Announcement *at a Sparta Rotterdam v Ajax match*

Please clear the pitch. (Louder) Please get off the pitch. (Louder still) Do not jump on the goalie, you numpty!
Announcement *at Sheffield United after fans celebrated play-off victory over Preston*

Can the people trying to break into the boardroom please be aware that you're on CCTV.
Announcement *at Mansfield Town*

The letters I get tend to start with things like 'Dear Stupid' or 'Dear Big Head'. One began 'Dear Alfie boy'.
Sir Alf Ramsey, *England manager, in 1968*

My favourite letter was one which said, 'You, Smith, Jones and Heighway had better keep looking over your shoulders. You're all going to get your dews.'
Emlyn Hughes, *Liverpool captain, on correspondence from Everton fans*

Savo [Milosevic] is the most one-footed player since Long John Silver.

Letter *to the* Birmingham Evening Mail

I went with two friends to watch Forest at Barnsley. It cost over £600 to watch the equivalent of what French farmers have been feeding their cattle.
Letter *to the* Nottingham Evening Post

The BBC should be banned from Ibrox. During the Dunfermline game the cameras showed me sitting in the Copland Stand when I was off work and on the sick.
Letter *to the Rangers fanzine* Follow, Follow

The only point worth remembering about Port Vale's match with Hereford on Monday was the fact that the attendance figure, 2,744, was a perfect cube, 14 x 14 x 14.
Letter *to Stoke-on-Trent's* Evening Sentinel

I don't know about weapons of mass destruction, but it takes Tottenham Hotspur only 45 minutes to turn a 3-0 lead into a 4-3 defeat against ten men. The thus-far fruitless search for their defence continues.
Letter *to* Guardian

Why the surprise over Argentina's elimination? When did a team with a large Scottish following ever qualify for the second round of the World Cup?

Letter *to the* Guardian *during the 2002 World Cup*

Einstein reckoned time slowed down the nearer a mass got to the speed of light. However, I have found an anomaly in this theory; I have called this the 'Ferguson paradox'. Time appears to alter at Old Trafford, depending on whether United need an equaliser, or a winner, when it seems to expand or contract. I call upon the Royal Society to investigate.
Letter *to* the Observer

First, Margaret Thatcher does her best to destroy the town. Now, Ben Thatcher viciously elbows our best crosser to destroy the team. Just what have they got against Sunderland?

Letter *to the* Sunderland Echo

May I wish Joe Royle well in a task equivalent to nailing jelly to a ceiling.

Letter *to the* Manchester Evening News *'Pink' after Royle beame Manchester City manager*

When manager Howard Wilkinson said Wednesday were only two players away from being a Championship-winning side, I didn't realise he meant Gullit and Maradona.

Letter *to the* Sheffield Green 'Un

Nottingham Playhouse hosted a David Platt in Conversation evening. Forest could make a fortune flogging the tapes to insomniacs.

Letter *to the* Daily Express

Is anyone else worried that Roy Keane's new bearded look is remarkably similar to the President of Iran, Mahmoud Ahmadinejad?

Letter *to the* Guardian

Perhaps as a pro-Europe gesture, we could give Beckham to the Spanish in exchange for keeping Gibraltar.
Letter *to* The Times *when Beckham joined Real Madrid*

They say football is a game of two halves. Not to me it isn't. I regularly down eight or nine pints while watching a live game on Sky TV in my local.
Letter *to* Viz *magazine*

I heard recently that, on average, Alex Ferguson receives two turds in the post each week. What I want to know is, who's sending the other one?
Letter *to* Viz *magazine*

I'm looking for a woman, but I keep landing on the same big old bloke.
Stuart Pearce, *Manchester City manager, on jumping into the crowd to celebrate goals*

I had death threats. When I received them, I wasn't too sure with some of them. A couple were written in crayon.

Martin Taylor *a year after his leg-break challenge on Arsenal's Eduardo*

You won't get me tuning in to a football phone-in, which are platforms for idiots. I'd rather listen to a game of chess on the radio.

Joe Royle

It will be a good day for burglars and the sheep will be left in peace.

Dick Campbell, *Brechin City manager, on a 'mass exodus' to a cup tie at Rangers*

The one thing I ask of a player before signing is 'Can you handle 35,000 crowds?' because you'll get stick. 'Oi, mate, you're fat, you've got big ears, a fat arse, a big hooter. You're ugly. I'll do your bird a favour if I see her down the pub.'

Alan Pardew, *West Ham manager*

I knew my days were numbered when I was warming up and one of our fans shouted: 'Kinnaird, we like the Poll Tax more than we like you.'

Paul Kinnaird *on playing for St Mirren*

Fidel Castro called the Cuban volleyball team's win over the US a sporting, psychological, patriotic and revolutionary history. At Stamford Bridge we're quite happy to settle for three points.

Sebastian Coe, *Chelsea fan*

Q: What's the craziest request you've had from a fan?
A: Can you do your brother's autograph?
Carl Hoddle, *Barnet midfielder.*

As an ex-Southampton player I'd normally have got stick from the Pompey fans, but I was helping them out in an injury crisis. They still sang 'We've got a Scummer in our goal', but with affection.
Dave Beasant

Ladies and gentlemen, we have stopped, overlooking the Tyne, so that Newcastle fans can throw themselves in the river.
Sunderland-supporting train driver *when Kevin Keegan left Newcastle in 1997*

INTERVIEWER: What's the worst thing anyone's ever said to you?
SEAN BEAN: Do you support Sheffield Wednesday?
Exchange *from a newspaper Q & A*

I've got a tattoo on my arm saying '100% Blade'. When we filmed the steamy scenes in *Lady Chatterley's Lover*, Ken Russell used to hide it with a strategically placed fern.
Sean Bean

Places like this [Sheffield United] are the soul of English football. The crowd is magnificent, singing 'F*** off Mourinho'.
José Mourinho

I come from a mixed marriage: Liverpool and Everton. There were always rucks. I can't believe my mum and dad are still together.
Peter Reid

The Glaswegian definition of an atheist is a bloke who goes to a Rangers-Celtic game to watch the football.
Sandy Strang, *Rangers fan, on a TV documentary*

For a while I did unite Celtic and Rangers fans. People in both camps hated me.
Mo Johnston *on playing for both Glasgow giants*

There was a jersey with a childish scrawl on it which read: 'To Saint Tommy, now up in heaven, please say hello to the rest of the Saints. Especially Saint Petersburg.'
Daily Telegraph *report after ex-Celtic manager Tommy Burns died shortly before Zenit St Petersburg beat Rangers in the UEFA Cup final*

Celtic have all the cool people supporting them. Rangers have me and Wet Wet Wet.
Alan McGee, *founder of Creation Records and ex-manager of Oasis*

To celebrate Arsenal's defeat in Europe, ten per cent off everything.
Advert *by World of Kosher food retailer in the* Jewish Chronicle

50% off dry cleaning from 16-23 May [1998] if Arsenal do the Double.
Advert *in the* Hampstead & Highgate Express

The accused claimed he was the reincarnated brother of Conan the Barbarian, that he was turning into an elk and had played for Leeds United. A defence psychiatrist said he was mad.
Court report *in the* Daily Telegraph

Man offers marriage proposal to any woman with ticket for Leeds v Sheffield United game. Must send photo (of ticket).
Advert *in the* Yorkshire Evening Post

The fans keep waiting for something to go wrong. I call it City-itis. It's a rare disease whose symptoms are relegation twice every three seasons.
Joe Royle, *Manchester City manager*

Our new guitarist and bassist have to have nice taste in shoes and a good haircut, and not be a Man United fan. If they can do that, they're sorted.
Liam Gallagher *of Oasis*

If we win the derby I'll jump off the stand roof with a parachute. Lose and I won't bother with the parachute.
Mike Summerbee, *ex-Manchester City player*

I inherited two fatal flaws from my father: premature baldness and Manchester City, neither of which I can change.
Howard Davies, *former deputy governor of the Bank of England*

Q: How many Man United fans does it take to change a lightbulb?
A: Three. One to change the bulb, one to buy the light-changing commemorative CD and one to drive the other two back to Devon.
Quick Quiz *in the* Sun

I told my lads if they signed for Man United they would have to keep their shirts in the garage.

Marcus Walmsley, *Leeds fan, on why his eight-year-old twins chose Leeds ahead of Manchester United*

Supporting a second team – in the Premier League – is like Yasser Arafat saying he has a soft spot for Judaism.
Nick Hancock, *TV personality and Stoke fan*

Our average away support is eight. We're the only football club where the players know all the fans by name.
Bill Perryman, *Yeading commercial director*

You can't turn a fire-extinguisher on fans. It'll only inflame the situation.

John Ball, *West Ham safety officer*

During the kerfuffle over Michael Heseltine's pit closures, Brian Clough led a march past my surgery, which is near the Nottingham Forest ground. Forest were heading for relegation at the time and I threatened to lead a counter demonstration past the ground.
Kenneth Clark MP

There are more hooligans in the House of Commons than at a football match.

Brian Clough

The English stick their psychos in Broadmoor, while the Welsh put theirs in Ninian Park.
Article about Cardiff fans in the Fulham fanzine One F in Fulham

Strongbow Cider – Helping fuel soccer riots for 40 years
Advert (quickly withdrawn) in the USA

Drinking alcohol can be dangerous as it leads to drunkenness.
Advice from a UEFA fans' handbook at Euro 2004

One supporters' club 'do' I used to attend started on the Saturday night and we stayed all Sunday and got home on Monday. We called it the equestrian because it was a three-day event.
Andy Goram, Rangers goalkeeper

Do you want your share of the gate money, or shall we just return the empties?
Bill Shankly to Jock Stein after fans threw bottles at Liverpool v Celtic

The Vikings knocked hell out of the Scots a thousand years ago, but we obviously taught them how to drink.
Norway fan *quoted in the French press at World Cup game v Scotland*

The Scotland fans' ability to smuggle drink into matches makes Papillon look like a learner.
Spokesman *for the Scottish Police Federation*

Most of the Tartan Army have woken up to the fact that wearing the kilt is the easiest way of attracting the opposite sex.
Haggis Supper, *Scotland fanzine*

It is the right of every Englishman to fall asleep if he wants, particularly if he is watching Arsenal.
Judge Michael Taylor *quashing a fan's conviction for drunkenness after he dozed off during a game*

It's bad enough having to watch Bristol City without having things stolen.
Judge Desmond Vowden QC *sentencing a man who stole from a City fan's car*

I must have done all right for the Birmingham fans to gob all over me.
Steve Jones, *Bournemouth player*

The Chelsea fans threw celery and sweetcorn at me when I went to take corners. It made me laugh to think of them popping into greengrocers' shops en route to Wembley.
Ryan Giggs

It's always great fun getting attacked. One of the highlights of my career. The guy got fined £100, but they had a whip-round in the pub and he got £200.

Gordon Strachan *recalls being attacked by a Celtic fan while playing*

The fans' pitch invasion was just high spirits. The only hooligans here are the players.

Dave Bassett, *Wimbledon manager*

One of the pitch invaders said I wouldn't get out of Millwall alive. Then he said I was fat. I said: 'Have you looked at yourself lately?'

Kevin Pressman, *Sheffield Wednesday goalkeeper*

My life changed after Brian [Clough] cuffed me. I was asked for my autograph, bus drivers gave me free rides, girls threw themselves at me and my old headmaster invited me to open the school fete.

Sean O'Hara, *Forest fan punched by the manager after invading the pitch*

If Eric Cantona had jumped into our crowd, he'd never have come out alive.

Alex Rae, *Millwall player*

At 6.45 the Millwall supporters were taken under escort towards the stadium. As they passed a public house, a group of 30 to 40 males came out, and bottles were thrown and pub windows smashed. After a while it became apparent that both groups were from Millwall and each thought the other were Bristol City supporters.

Report *from the National Criminal Intelligence Unit*

They should make Leeds play all their away matches at home.

Billy Hamilton, *Oxford striker, after visiting Leeds fans rioted*

I expected abuse but I also got a hamburger and about £4.50 in change.

Gary Neville *after objects were thrown at him at Liverpool*

When I called Coventry supporters a bunch of wankers, it was the best 15 grand I ever spent.

Ian Wright *on being fined*

The fans who gave me stick are the ones who still point at aeroplanes.

Ian Wright

The people chanting 'Taylor out!' were the ones singing 'Graham, give us a wave' when we were two up at Everton.

Graham Taylor *at Aston Villa*

I loved everything about the job, even the chants of 'Sit down Pinnochio'.

Phil Thompson, *former assistant manager of Liverpool*

Those fans who don't get behind the team should shut the hell up or they can come round to my house and I will fight them.

Ian Holloway, *QPR manager*

We do have the greatest fans in the world, but I've never seen a fan score a goal.

Jock Stein, *Scotland manager*

Call that ten yards, ref? I wouldn't let you measure my carpets.

Blyth Spartans fan *at the 2009 FA Cup tie against Blackburn*

Adrian attends Bromley Comprehensive and is a keen goalkeeper. He likes listening to music and playing computer games. His favourite players have left the club.

Profile *of the mascot in the Crystal Palace programme*

The Archbishop has broad musical taste, from Elgar and Bach to Genesis and Supertramp. He also supports Arsenal, but nobody's perfect.

Brian Pearson, *secretary to Archbishop of Canterbury Dr George Carey*

Glenn Hoddle is supposed to have heard us and said 'I want that band'. He actually said 'I want them banned'.

Laurence Garraty, *trumpeter in the Sheffield Wednesday Kop Band, on being invited to play at England games*

Can anything be done about entertaining us after the kick-off?

Stoke supporter *interrupting a debate about pre-match entertainment at the club's AGM*

A true football fan is one who knows the nationality of every player in the Republic of Ireland team.

Ken Bolam, *musician*

I made a two-finger gesture to the Port Vale fans to show I'd scored twice, and that must've been misinterpreted.

Paul Peschisolido *on a hostile reception playing for West Brom*

Q: What question are you most asked by fans?
A: Why are you bald?

Kevin Russell, *Wrexham player, answering a* Sun *questionnaire*

If it had been one of our meat pies it would have done more damage than a brick.

Andy Ritchie, *Oldham manager, after a fan threw a pie at the referee*

Boys enter here: Admission 3d. Boys with whiskers – Two turnstiles up: Admission 6d.

Sign *at Oldham Athletic in 1910*

I thought I'd heard it all when it comes to the fickleness of football fans. Then I heard the Spurs fans singing: 'There's only one Alan Sugar.'

Mick McCarthy

If a giant time machine were invented, the Manchester United sales staff would be the first on it. They would sell replica shirts to the Romans as soon as they landed in Britain.

Colin Shindler, *Manchester City-supporting writer*

If you want farce, comedy or pantomime, go to Newcastle. It's been that way since 1947.

Sid Waddell, *darts commentator and Newcastle fan, in 2008*

Our new strip looks like it was designed by Julian Clary with a migraine.

Sean Bean, *actor and Sheffield United supporter*

When I first heard about Viagra I thought it was a new player Chelsea had signed.

Tony Banks MP, *Minister for Sport and Chelsea supporter*

If only our club motto, 'No battle, no victory', wasn't taken so literally.

Mark Staniforth, *Scarborough supporter, in the* Independent

I make all sorts of excuses at work to avoid missing a Burnley game. I've had several aunties die in a season. After a game with Norwich was rained off, my boss said: 'I see your aunt's funeral was postponed due to a waterlogged pitch.'

Dave Burnley, *Staffordshire-based fan who changed his surname by deed poll*

The fans are mugs. Newcastle girls are dogs. Me, I like blondes, big bust, good legs. I don't like coloured girls. I want a lesbian show with handcuffs.

Freddy Shepherd, *Newcastle chairman, secretly taped by the* News of the World

United fans come up to me and say, 'Thanks for giving me the best night of my life.' They usually add: 'But please don't tell the wife.'

Ole Gunnar Solskjaer *on his 1999 Champions League-winning goal*

Every thousandth person created, God unhinges their heads, scoops out their brains and then issues them to a football club as supporters.

Mike Bateson, *Torquay chairman*

11: 'Trouble with the missus': The WAGs

Me and Wilf McGuinness both got the sack from Manchester United, but to this day I don't know whose wife Wilf was seeing.
Tommy Docherty, *sacked after his relationship with the wife of United's physio became known*

I told the players that they might never get the opportunity to reach a big final again, so they should go out there and do it for their wives, girlfriends – or both for that matter.
Paul Jewell *at Wigan*

I didn't have a chip at Ashley [Cole]. He's in enough trouble with the missus when she gets home.

Clinton Morrison, *Coventry striker, on facing the Chelsea defender after his drunken night out while wife Cheryl was climbing Mount Kilimanjaro for Comic Relief*

John Bond has blackened my name with his insinuations about the private lives of football managers. Both my wives are upset.

Malcolm Allison

Girls have sent me suggestive pictures and said what they would like to do to me. I'm absolutely shocked by their suggestions. Then I get my girlfriend Sarah to act them out.

James Beattie, *Southampton striker*

David wearing a sarong is nothing out of the ordinary. He wears my knickers as well.

Victoria Beckham

I've read the new biography of David from cover to cover and it's got some nice pictures.

Victoria Beckham

With my 'DB' tattoo, I'd have to marry David Blaine or Daniel Bedingfield if we split up.

Victoria Beckham

David is very, very tidy and I am not. Even our fridge is colour-coded. He vacuums in straight lines, in a pinny. And if anyone walks around after he's done it, he gets funny.
Victoria Beckham

One woman turned up at my place every day for two weeks and left different pairs of underpants in the mailbox. Luckily they were always brand new.
David Beckham *on life in Madrid*

It has always been my greatest dream to have sex on the roof of Real's Santiago Bernabeu stadium in my favourite city, Madrid.
Nives Celcius*, wife of Croatian midfielder Dino Drpic*

I've gone from whore to nun in five minutes.
Joaquín Caparrós*, Athletic Bilbao coach, on fast-changing public perceptions*

It's incredible that my girlfriend has left me. Only recently I paid £7,000 to have her breasts enlarged, and now this.
Mo Idrissou*, Hanover striker*

Dennis Wise grabbed my tit. I had five finger marks around the nipple, like a love bite. That took some explaining to the missus.
Jason McAteer *recalls a Liverpool v Chelsea clash*

Q: What do you set the video for?
A: It has to be *Footballers' Wives*. I like the show's gritty realism.
Iffy Onura*, Sheffield United striker, in a programme interview*

I've sold my wedding pictures – to *The Kop* magazine for a quid.
Jamie Carragher on the WAG culture

Tell the WAGs we've got a brand new shopping centre in Plymouth.
Ian Holloway, Plymouth manager.

If you've been out for a night and you're looking for a young lady and you pull one, some weeks they're good-looking and some weeks they're not the best. Our performance would have been not the best-looking bird, but at least we got her in a taxi. She weren't the best-looking lady we've ended up taking home, but she was very pleasant, so thanks very much and let's have a coffee.
Ian Holloway after his QPR team won

I didn't cry at my wedding or the birth of my children, so my wife has warned me there will be trouble if we get promoted and she sees a tear in my eye.

Marc Bircham before playing for QPR in the play-off final

My wife said I looked good in hoops. After QPR there weren't that many options.
Bircham on joining Yeovil, who wear green and white hoops

Q: Biggest thrill of your life?
A: When my wife told me she was pregnant and signing for Newcastle.
Albert Craig answers a Sun questionnaire

It was his weekend off. He can do what he wants. Do you spend time with your girlfriend? Do you go to the cinema with her? Would you like her to kiss you now and then? That's what Artur [Boruc] has done. I still go to the cinema with my wife. I still kiss her. She doesn't like it, but there you go.
Gordon Strachan, Celtic manager, after his goalkeeper was seen out on the town

Trying to explain it [Celtic's defeat by St Mirren] to you would be impossible. It would be like you trying to explain childbirth to me.
Gordon Strachan to radio reporter Michelle Evans, who had not had children

MANAGER (TO PAUNCHY PLAYER): If that stomach was on a player, she'd be pregnant.
PLAYER: It was, and she is.
Dressing-room exchange related by Craig Brown, former Scotland manager

Three weeks ago I'd never heard of Alan Shearer. Now I want to have his babies.

Lynne Truss, The Times. She later 'grew to hate him'

My wife cringes every time someone calls me Sir Alex or calls her Lady Cathy. She says: 'I don't know why you accepted it in the first place.'
Sir Alex Ferguson

The cook prepares very good food. I prefer to stay here and eat rather than going to my house. But don't tell my wife.

Gianfranco Zola *at West Ham*

I took my wife out on Saturday night but all I was thinking about was our back four. It was like taking the back four out as well.
Roy Keane *at Sunderland*

It takes a lot to get me excited. Ask my wife.
Roy Keane

I used to think I'd like to have met my wife 30 years ago, until I realised she'd be minus four.
George Best

There's no better feeling in the world than to win in the last minute, though your wife might disagree.
Martin Jol *at Tottenham*

I go now on holiday for the next three hours then work again. My children are in school and my wife would like to divorce me because I told her she can go alone on the holiday as I am here to work.

Csaba László, *Hearts manager*

I'll have my mobile on holiday with me and as long as my wife doesn't find it, I'll continue to work. If she does find it, maybe she will throw it into the swimming pool.

Rafael Benitez

How can you tell your wife that you're just popping out to play a match and then not come back for five days?

Rafael Benitez *on Test cricket*

When I first met my wife and told her I was a footballer, she said, 'Yes, but what do you do for a living?'

Christian Karembeu, *France midfielder*

If I told my wife I was considering becoming a manager, she'd say, 'Sign this then. Don't worry, it's only a divorce. Au revoir.'

David Ginola

A manager has to be a bit of a social worker these days. If Claire Rayner knew football, she'd be a great manager.
Mick McCarthy

I used to stand up and glare around when people gave Geoff stick. Norman Hunter's mum lashed out with her handbag when people booed her Norman.
Judith Hurst, *wife of England World Cup hat-trick hero Geoff*

Last thing at night Bill [Shankly] takes the dog for a walk on Everton's training ground. The poor animal is not allowed back until he has done his business.
Nessie Shankly

Death threats? The only threats I've had this week have been from the wife for not doing the washing up.

Harry Redknapp *before managing Southampton against his old club Portsmouth*

I had so much trouble sleeping that for a while I was addicted to Night Nurse. When I told [wife] Sandra she thought I was talking about some bird in suspenders.
Harry Redknapp *on how losing affects him*

I was in bed with my wife last night – if you're as ugly as me you want to talk about football – and she said: 'Harry, if you're drawing, push Trevor Sinclair up front.' So I gambled and it worked.

Harry Redknapp *at West Ham*

The police searched my house and took away a computer that I bought my wife two years ago. I think she only learned to turn it on four weeks ago.

Harry Redknapp *under investigation for corruption*

We've got a poor home record against Man United? In that case I probably won't come to the game. My wife wanted to go Christmas shopping so I'll probably go to Woolworths.

Harry Redknapp *when Woolworths was on the verge of collapse*

My wife Jane told me: 'If you don't get a result, your bags will be packed and at the front door.' And she wasn't kidding.

Brian Laws, *Sheffield Wednesday manager, after winning the derby against United*

My wife was hoping I'd get the sack so we could retire down to Cornwall with the children.

Neil Warnock *at Sheffield United*

The reason I'm back in football is that the wife wants me out of the house.

Kenny Dalglish *on becoming Blackburn manager*

We interrupt this marriage to bring you the football season.
Slogan *on a mug in the kitchen of Kenny and Marina Dalglish*

Me and the missus sat down last night, put the players' names in a hat and drew them out.
Stuart Pearce *after Nottingham Forest won his first game as acting manager*

Whether or not we beat Germany, I will stay away from you all for seven days. I have to sleep with my wife.
Luiz Felipe Scolari, *Brazil coach, to the media before the 2002 World Cup final*

My wife made me delete the clip from the Sky + after four days.
Chris Iwelumo *after missing an 'open goal' for Scotland against Norway*

Of course I didn't take my wife to watch Rochdale as a present for our wedding anniversary. It was her birthday. Would I have got married during the football season? And anyway it wasn't Rochdale, it was Rochdale reserves.
Bill Shankly

Retire? That wife of mine bullies me. She throws me out of the door at seven o'clock every morning. I daren't risk the wrath of that lass from the Gorbals.
Sir Alex Ferguson

You can always tell how a team is doing by the state of the wives. Second Division wives always need roots touching up.
Mrs Merton, *played by Caroline Aherne*

When I said even my missus could save Derby from relegation, I was exaggerating.
Peter Taylor

My idea of relaxation: Going somewhere away from the wife.

Terry Fenwick, *QPR captain*

Most dangerous opponent: My ex-wife.
Frank Worthington

Q: Craziest request you've had from a fan?
A: What's your wife's phone number and when's your next away game?
Francis Benali, *Southampton defender*

I loved football and playing morning and afternoon. Even when I went to bed with my wife I was training.
Diego Maradona

If it wasn't for Tracey, I'd be an 18 stone bricklayer playing for Penicuik Athletic.
Andy Goram *on his second wife*

Andy Goram and Miriam Wylie split after less than two years of marriage when she found a woman's footprints on the ceiling of their Shogun 4x4.
Report *in the* Scottish Sun

The centre-forward [his son Nigel] isn't joining Pisa for the simple and most important reason that his mother decided that days ago.
Brian Clough

Our husbands think we're shopping in Dublin.
Banner *at Portugal v Republic of Ireland in Lisbon*

Why didn't you just belt the ball?
Barbara Southgate *to son Gareth after his penalty shoot-out miss put England out of Euro 96*

My son having a romance with a weather girl? I spoke to him and he talked about the weather but not a weather girl.
Ulla Eriksson, *Sven's mother, on reports of his affair with Ulrika Jonsson*

Not everyone was captivated by the England-Argentina match. My wife fell asleep during the penalty shoot-out.
Letter *to the* Daily Telegraph

I did a 24-hour sponsored silence for Children In Need and if I hadn't had my girlfriend to talk to, I think I would have struggled.
Anton Ferdinand, *Sunderland defender*

You can go to nice restaurants but you can't beat fish and chips, can you? My girlfriend Stacey is the same. Of course she likes nice clothes but she isn't one who likes to go to posh restaurants. She goes where I go – I am the boss.
David Wheater, *Middlesbrough defender*

If Harry misses a goal, the Leeds fans shout: 'You're keeping him up too long – stop shagging him!'

Sheree Murphy, Emmerdale *actress, on her soon-to-be husband Harry Kewell*

His girlfriend doesn't want to live in Brum. I've told him to change his girlfriend and not his club.

Barry Fry *on Birmingham's Portuguese winger José Dominguez*

How can women referees make accurate decisions if they have never been tackled from behind by a 14-stone centre-half, elbowed in the ribs, or even caught offside?

Joe Royle *at Manchester City*

Every club has three types – fans, parasites and people who work their bollocks off, even ladies.

Ken Bates, *Leeds chairman*

I haven't laughed so much since Ma caught her tits in a mangle.

Ken Bates, *Leeds chairman, in a dispute with his previous club, Chelsea*

When I played for Forest at Derby they were chucking coins and spitting at me when I took the throw-ins. And that was just the old ladies.

Stuart Pearce

I love to be around people who are prepared to kick their granny.
John Gregory, *Queens Park Rangers manager*

If it meant getting three points on a Saturday I'd shoot my grandmother. Not nastily – I would just hurt her.
Brian Clough

Could Scott Brown please come to the crèche – your girlfriend is here and this game is boring.

Public address *announcement at Hearts*

If Frank McAvennie's catchphrase is 'Where's the burdz?' then my answer has to be 'in hiding' because he's revolting.
Katie Price *aka Jordan, model and TV celebrity, on the former Scotland striker*

I've always believed in treating the ball like a woman. Give it a cuddle, caress it a wee bit, take your time, and you'll get the desired response.
Jim Baxter

I hate football as most women do. I prefer the indoor sort of games.
Cynthia Payne, *Streatham 'madam'*

The court said it was unusual for a man to complain about his wife spending too much time on football.
Wendy Toms, *referee, on her divorce*

Footballers are only interested in drinking, clothes and the size of their willies.
Karren Brady

[Jamie] Carragher had a big mouth, about the only thing about him that was big.

Liz Traill, stripper, after Carragher went naked at Liverpool's Christmas party

Statistics are like mini-skirts. They give you good ideas but they hide the most important things.
Ebbe Skovdahl, Aberdeen manager

No wonder that girl [Antonia De Sancha] was licking David Mellor's toes. She was probably trying to get as far away from his face as possible.
Tommy Docherty

Charles [Saatchi] dreamt I had an affair with Steve Coppell. I said to him: 'Thanks a lot. You might have made it Mourinho.'
Nigella Lawson

I didn't get too many women running after me. It was their f*****g husbands who'd be after me.
Charlie George

I will tell you straight away, before you ask: I have never slept with a footballer, never gone to dinner with one and never seen one naked in the shower. OK. Now we can start.

Paola Ferrera, *Italian TV football presenter, before being interviewed*

Q: Who's your dream woman?
A: Jennifer Lopez with the personality of Kathy Burke.

Jason McAteer *in a newspaper interview*

We know Arsene Wenger likes the look of Arshavin. But I like the look of Angelina Jolie; it doesn't always mean you get what you want.

Dennis Lachter, *agent to Russia striker Andrei Arshavin*

Which Spanish club did John Toshack take over after leaving Sporting Lesbian?

Quiz question *in the Leek Town programme*

Arsenal Ladies have won the league – credit to them for showing more balls than their male counterparts.

Tony Cascarino

I never expected to get the man-of-the-match award.

Lesley Shipp, *Arsenal Ladies player*

You couldn't beat our ladies.
Chant *by Arsenal fans to Tottenham before a 4-1 lead became a 4-4 draw*

Arsenal Ladies would do really well [against Tottenham's men]. I'm sure they would get a point.
Cesc Fabregas *in* Loaded *magazine before Arsenal drew with Spurs*

Trollops on Tour.
Sign *in the Manchester United Ladies team bus*

When I wear skirts people say: 'Oh my God, I didn't know you had legs.' What do they think I play football with every week?
Marianne Spacey, *Fulham player-coach*

There's not a word to describe how I feel, but I'm ecstatic.
Mary Philip, *Arsenal women's player, after winning the UEFA Cup*

12: 'Going missing': Sex & drink & rock 'n' roll

Q: What would you be if you hadn't become a footballer?
A: A virgin.

Peter Crouch interviewed

In 1969 I gave up alcohol and women. It was the worst 20 minutes of my life.

George Best

A blonde girl arrived and said, 'My car's broken down outside your house. Can I use your phone to call the AA?' I had her on the carpet in the hallway, gave her a quick repair job before the AA man arrived.

George Best

I've always had a reputation for going missing – Miss England, Miss UK, Miss World.

George Best

I spent a lot of my money on birds, booze and fast cars. The rest I just squandered.

George Best

MICHAEL PARKINSON: What was the nearest to kick-off time that you made love?
GEORGE BEST: Er... I think it was half-time actually.

Exchange on Parkinson's chat show

People always say I shouldn't be burning the candle at both ends. Maybe because they haven't got a big enough candle.

George Best

If you'd given me a choice between beating four defenders and smashing in a goal from 30 yards or going to bed with Miss World, it would have been difficult. Luckily I did both. It's just that you do one of those things in front of 50,000 people.

George Best

The Queen was quite a stunner in her youth. Who knows what might have happened if I'd met her in Tramp in my heyday.
George Best

If I were reincarnated I'd come back as George Best, because he was a genius and had all them women and drank all that wine.
Barry Fry

His team-mates called him Gigolo. Unfortunately it took me a while to cotton on to the full significance of the nickname.
Alex Best *on dating former Tottenham defender John Scales*

David is an animal in bed. Some woman asked me in an interview: 'Are you so thin because you shag all day?' I said: 'Actually, yes.'
Victoria Beckham

I've no idea how long [the sex] lasted. When you're in bed with David Beckham, you're not looking at the clock.

Sarah Marbeck, *who claimed an affair with Beckham*

Beckham has the face of an angel and the bum of a Greek god. Rumour has it his tackle is enough not only to take your breath away but possibly do you serious damage.
Attitude, *gay magazine*

I shook Sean Connery's hand. That hand has been on so many pairs of boobs.
Paul Gascoigne

Q: What's more satisfying, scoring a hat-trick or having great sex?
A: The missus might read this, so I'd better say the sex.
Kevin Phillips *interviewed by* Loaded *magazine*

Les [Ferdinand] loved sex but always checked the football results on Teletext first.

Eva Dijkstra, *model*

The bellboy was my friend and he would bring girls up to my room. When I'd finished with them, he would take them off me on the stairs and hand me a pastry. Sex and cakes, the perfect night.
Antonio Cassano, *Italy striker on life at Real Madrid*

Our home form is poor. Maybe my players are having a rampant sex life when they stay at home on Friday nights.
Terry Burton, *Wimbledon manager*

Football is a fertility festival. Eleven sperm trying to get into the egg. I feel sorry for the goalkeeper.
Björk

Football is a permanent orgasm.
Claude Le Roy, *Cameroon coach*

If we beat Real, it will be a nationwide orgasm.

Jesus Gil, *Atletico Madrid president*

We play what I call 'orgy football'. The other team know they're going to get it, but they don't know from whom or where from.
Sam Hammam, *Cardiff City chairman*

Footballers come high up the list now in terms of shagability. Rock stars must still be first, but then it's footballers, then actors, firemen, insurance brokers, then TV quiz-show hosts.
Angus Deayton

The average English footballer couldn't tell the difference between an attractive woman and a corner flag.
Walter Zenga, *Italy goalkeeper*

The pressure of managing Walsall has been so great that I've stopped having sex.

Ray Graydon

I'm off home to give my wife a big hug, because I doubt if I can manage anything else.

Luiz Felipe Scolari *after a draining win for Portugal over Spain*

With the luck we've been having, one of our players must be bonking a witch.

Ken Brown, *Norwich manager*

The reason I don't employ my brothers is knowing how the players would react if I turned up one day and said: 'I'd like you to meet Cock and Dick.'

Martin Jol, *Tottenham manager*

There have been rumours about players sleeping with each other's wives, but it isn't true. We're all pulling together.

Fabian Wilnis, *Ipswich defender*

I've played Eggert Jonsson in so many positions this season that, if it wasn't football, it would be sexual assault.

Csaba László, *Hearts manager*

Sex could never be as rewarding as winning the World Cup. Not that sex isn't great, but this tournament comes around only every four years and sex is a lot more regular than that.

Ronaldo *after winning the World Cup in 2002*

I couldn't hope to emulate David Mellor, since the days of Jimmy Greaves, it's the first time anyone has scored five times in a Chelsea shirt.

Tony Banks, *Minister for Sport, on his fellow supporter's alleged sexual exploits*

My girlfriend won't be happy to hear I've been chasing Totti around Rome.

Jonathan Woodgate *before a Roma v Leeds match*

I get propositioned sometimes, which is nice. My mates love it – they get all the cast-offs.

Mark Burchill *when he was a 19-year-old Celtic striker*

He loved my boobs almost brushing his face. I could feel his Brazilian breath panting on them.

Lisa Collins, *lap-dancer, claiming eight-times nightly sex with Ronaldinho*

I'm so unlucky that if I fell into a wheelbarrow of boobs I'd come out sucking my thumb.

Ian Holloway *at QPR*

We play every three days. How can I be a good husband if I don't make love before each game?

Franck Leboeuf

To this World Cup I've brought my football boots and inflatable doll, because a month without a woman would be difficult.

Eric Deflandre, *Belgium defender*

We are told we cannot have women in the camp. This policy is supposed to make us world champions. Of what? Masturbation?

Luis Pereira, *Brazil player at the 1974 World Cup*

Let the wives into the camp! Love is good for the players, as long as it's not at half-time.

Richard Moller Nielsen, *Denmark coach at Euro 92 – which the Danes won*

Sex before a game? The boys can do what they like. But it's not possible at half-time.

Berti Vogts, *Germany coach*

It's not the sex that tires out young players. It's staying up all night looking for it.

Clemens Westerhof, *Nigeria manager*

We don't want them to be monks. We want them to be football players, because monks don't play football at that level.

Sir Bobby Robson *on reports of Newcastle players being seen in nightclubs*

I promised the boys a hamper full of caviar and Viagra and I think it must have worked.

Mohamed Al Fayed, *Fulham owner, after his team escaped relegation*

I haven't a clue exactly how many women I had [on holiday in Ayia Napa] – four or five maybe. But I regret it deeply.

Kieron Dyer

I'm so exciting that every time I play, the fans want to have sex with me.

Paolo Di Canio *at West Ham*

When I was with Norwich my wife Dawn had a baby and we called her Darby. A month later I joined Derby. The Norwich lads are all trying for babies and they're going to call them Lazio or Barcelona.

Ashley Ward

I have been reborn because of my faith. I'm an evangelical now. I have not had sex for two years now. There's nothing going on down there. Really.

Nicola Legrottaglie, *Juventus player*

Hump it, bump it, whack. That may be a recipe for a good sex life, but it won't win us the World Cup.

Ken Bates *after Graham Taylor's direct style failed to take England to the finals*

Playing against a team with no attacking intent is like making love to a tree.

Jorge Valdano, *Real Madrid official*

We're like soft porn right now. There's an awful lot of foreplay and not an awful lot going on in the box.

Keith Hill, *Rochdale manager*

I remember telling one of my previous team that I could murder sausage and chips. He looked at me and said: 'I should think you get enough sausage already, don't you?'

Paul Barker, *captain of gay London team Stonewall*

DES O'CONNOR: If England win the World Cup, will you come back and sing a duet with me?
ELTON JOHN: If they win, I'll come back and sleep with you.

Exchange *on O'Connor's chat show in 1998*

I started the shirt-lifting thing and I'm still the best at it.

Fabrizio Ravanelli *struggles with his English idioms*

The girls like Lampsy. If I was that way, I'd see something in him.

John Terry *on Frank Lampard*

Q: Does the thought of facing Ronaldo give you nightmares?
A: No. I never dream about him. He's not really my type.
Colin Hendry *in an exchange with a Brazilian journalist*

Dani is so good-looking that Villa didn't know whether to mark him or bonk him.
Harry Redknapp *on a Portuguese signing*

Last year I got more Valentines cards off blokes than off girls. They write love poems. It's scary.
Matt Jansen, *Blackburn striker*

Our defence was a wall of real men facing Valencia's homosexuals.

Alejandro Lago *of Norway's Rosenborg Trondheim*

In the papers this morning they said the nation's thoughts were on Michael Owen's groin. I thought, Me too!
Graham Norton

Did you know that Ronaldo is great at imitating queers?

Ze Carlos, *Brazil team-mate*

One night we went out in Bangkok and there were transsexuals everywhere. Everybody fancied them because they were absolutely gorgeous. They'd be playing with your cock under the table and it was like living in a different world.

Mel Sterland

It's a pleasure to be standing up here. It's a pleasure to be standing up.

George Best *accepts the Footballer of the Century award*

I'd give all the champagne I've ever drunk to have played with Eric Cantona on a big European night at Old Trafford.

George Best

Kevin Keegan is not fit to lace George Best's drinks.

John Roberts, *sports journalist*

They said Bestie was roaring drunk on the Parkinson show but Oliver Reed phoned the BBC to say: 'He looks all right to me.'

Frank Worthington

There weren't any celebrities or footballers there. It was just him and his family getting pissed.

Kelly Jones *of Stereophonics after playing at the wedding reception for Wayne Rooney and Colleen McLoughlin*

I thought he [Glenn Hoddle] said, 'Do you want to visit a brewery?' but it turned out he asked if I'd like to see [faith healer] Eileen Drewery.

Paul Gascoigne

I didn't know Walter [Smith], but I knew he must be Scottish because I saw him carrying big discount cases of lager back from the supermarket.

Paul Gascoigne *on first seeing his soon-to-be Rangers manager in Florida*

For Tony Adams to admit he's an alcoholic takes an enormous amount of bottle.

Ian Wright

Tony Adams is appealing. Apparently he wasn't pissed, just trying to get the wall back ten yards.

Bob 'The Cat' Bevan *when Adams was charged with drink-driving after crashing into a wall*

If there were a World Drinking XI, Pelé would have the No. 10 shirt.

Alan Hudson

One or two players would like the competition renamed the Vodka and Coca-Cola Cup.

Ron Atkinson

Q: Who has been the biggest influence on your career?
A: IAN ST JOHN: Bill Shankly.
A: JIMMY GREAVES: Vladimir Smirnov.
Interview in Loaded *magazine*

I can drink like a chimney.
Duncan Ferguson

Some of the younger players think that lager makes you invisible.
Craig Brown, *Scotland manager.*

The jack the lads who go to the pub after games are not my cup of tea.

Tommy McLean, *Dundee United manager*

I don't want angels in my team – they can get out of their brains every night as long as they're man of the match on Saturday.
John Gregory *at Aston Villa*

Everyone at Kilmarnock drinks industrial quantities of beer. One time the whole squad went on a trip to Newcastle. Everybody bought themselves animal costumes as though it was a carnival and we put them on to go on a pub crawl round the city. I was dressed as a cow.
Manuel Pascali, *Italian midfielder*

We'll still be happy if we lose. The match is on at the same time as the Munich Beer Festival.
Noel O'Mahoney, *Cork City manager, before a European tie against Bayern*

When [Czech defender] Dusan Vrto first arrived, all he could say was 'yes', 'no' and 'morning'. A week later he had added 'thank you' and 'a Budweiser, please'.
Jim Duffy, *Dundee manager*

When we played his son Darren's team, Peterborough, Sir Alex [Ferguson] drank all my red wine, which I wasn't too pleased about.
Paul Ince *at Milton Keynes Dons*

Now that José [Mourinho] has gone I don't know what I'm going to do with all my wine.
Sir Alex Ferguson

I'm going to go out and get lambasted on wine.
Martin O'Neill *after Leicester won the League Cup*

We will worry about the final later. Now is the time for wine and cigarettes!

Klaus Toppmöller, *Bayer Leverkusen coach, after beating Manchester United to reach the Champions League final*

People will say – and they're absolutely right – that instead of walking on water I should have taken more of it with my drinks.
Brian Clough

I went in [to see Clough] shaking with fear to ask for a pay rise. I accepted a whisky and a wage cut.

Martin O'Neill

REPORTER: When do you stop thinking about relegation and start contemplating Europe?
PAUL JEWELL: After about ten pints.
Exchange in a TV interview as Jewell's Wigan side reached the Premiership's top six

Of all the honours I won, the one that pleased me most was when the House of Commons voted me Beer Drinker of the Year.
Jack Charlton

The only relaxed manager is Big Ron Atkinson. He had me drinking pink champagne – before the match.
Harry Redknapp

Scottish players booze, smoke and eat whatever comes to hand.
Jean Luc Wetzel, French agent.

I was terrified of Jock Stein. He even frowned on Coca-Cola. If he spotted you sneaking a Coke to your room at night, he'd throw it down the sink and say: 'I'll Coca-Cola you.'
Lou Macari *on his playing days at Celtic*

Q: Favourite drink?
A: Beer. No, I mean Coke.
Q: Most prized possession?
A: My car.
Eirik Bakke, *Leeds midfielder, in a programme interview before a drink-driving conviction*

Q: Last tin you opened?
A: Not tin. Bottle of wine.
Marcel Desailly *in a Chelsea programme feature*

Drink lots of beer and smoke loads of fags.
Gerry Taggart *gives advice to aspiring players*

People say our pre-season training has been gruelling, but if you left it to the players they would take a fortnight in Tenerife, the same in Cyprus and two more in the pub.
David Sullivan, *co-owner of Birmingham City*

I've raised the white flag with English food, and when I refused a beer my team-mates looked at me as if I were an alien.
Rolando Bianchi, *Italian striker with Manchester City*

Most of the Italian players nip into the toilets for a crafty fag at half-time.
Paul Gascoigne *at Lazio*

My only problem is with Italian breakfasts. No matter how much money you've got, you can't seem to get any Rice Krispies.
Luther Blissett *on joining AC Milan from Watford*

Gabriel Batistuta was a snob. He was Argentinian but acted really posh. One day at training we were queuing at the bar, he pushed in front of me. We were both getting a coffee macchiato. So I stuck a finger up my nose and stirred his drink with it, like it was a spoon.
Antonio Cassano, *Sampdoria player*

We eat a lot of McDonald's, where you have Ronald McDonald. So we chose the name Ronald for our baby son.
Ronaldo

Before every game I usually go to Burger King or McDonald's – very good for the hamstring.

Patrice Evra

If I go into a restaurant I'm thinking, He knows what I'm eating. Will I order chips or not?
Steven Taylor, *Newcastle defender, on interim manager Alan Shearer*

I'm nicknamed Trigger after the character in *Only Fools and Horses* because I'm basically thick. It came about in my Liverpool days when a waitress asked if I wanted my pizza cut into four pieces or eight. I said four because there was no way I could eat eight.
Jason McAteer

Q: If you had to live on only one type of food, what would it be?
A: A Domino's pepperoni pizza.
Dean Ashton, *West Ham striker, interviewed*

I'm great at romantic meals. I can only make baked beans and Pot Noodle so I buy a takeaway, pile up some dirty pans and serve it up so it looks like I've cooked it.
Matt Jansen, *Blackburn striker*

What a complete chicken nugget with double barbecue sauce he is.

Ian Holloway on Plymouth defender Paul Connolly

The new manager [Arsene Wenger] has put me on grilled fish, grilled broccoli, grilled everything. Yuk!
Ian Wright on initial resistance to Wenger at Arsenal

Can you follow a player home to check if his missus is giving him steak and kidney pie instead of pasta?
Harry Redknapp on players' diets

If you can't kick a ball straight, a plate of pasta ain't gonna help you.

Harry Redknapp

When we went to Wolves they put out a plate of sandwiches in the dressing room afterwards and I advised the players to eat as much as they could. We have to send someone out to find cheap food at Sainsbury's.

Steve Coppell at Crystal Palace

So far the only feedback I've had off the chairman is him asking me: 'Do you want a pie?'

Steve Bruce at Wigan Athletic

SUPPORTER: What's your favourite pie filling?
PAUL MERSON: I'm a Londoner and we don't have pies.

Exchange at Walsall's meet-the-manager forum

The main thing I miss about London? The sausages.

Terry Venables in Barcelona

Chelsea were a sausage, eggs and chips club before the foreign players arrived. That's what we ate before training and even before matches.

Dennis Wise

There's no question of our playing for a draw. As we say in Germany: 'We'll be going for the sausages.'
Jurgen Rober, *Hertha Berlin coach, before facing Chelsea*

Early on, one of the guys posed me a question – 'Ereyergoin-fersumscran?' I later understood that this was a polite invitation to go to lunch.
Brad Friedel, *Aston Villa's American goalkeeper*

Even the chef in our canteen has been out for two weeks with a hernia.
Alan Curbishley *during an injury crisis at West Ham*

Chris Coleman has the look of a celebrity chef about him.

Charlton *programme article*

At a French club they buy you champagne and cake on your birthday. Here they shove your face in the mud.
Franck Leboeuf *at Chelsea*

I couldn't believe it... F*****g cheese sandwiches an hour and a half before training.
Roy Keane *with the Ireland squad before the 2002 World Cup*

The Norway squad's eating habits surprised me, especially mixing jam with smoked fish or mackerel with bananas.
Georges-Marie Duffaud, *French hotelier, during the 1998 World Cup*

There are three types of Oxo cubes. Light brown for chicken stock, dark brown for beef stock and light blue for laughing stock.

Tommy Docherty on Manchester City

There's more important things to think about than what Augustin Delgado is saying in the papers. I've got a yoghurt in the fridge to finish, and the expiry date is today.

Gordon Strachan at Southampton

I took a pay cut to go to Coventry. As long as the fridge is full, I'm happy.

Gordon Strachan

Not so long ago he was working in a kitchen as a chef, so he has the hunger.

Aidy Boothroyd, Watford manager, on goalkeeper Ben Foster

We want our chocolate back.

Song by Arsenal players on the team bus after Arsene Wenger banned sugar

I wouldn't quote Kipling to the players. They would probably think I was talking about cakes.

Rob Kelly, Leicester manager

The only decisions I'm making at the moment are whether I have tea, coffee, toast or cornflakes in the morning.
Sam Allardyce *after being sacked as Newcastle manager*

You can't compare English and German football. They're like omelette and muesli.
Erik Meijer *after joining Hamburg from Liverpool*

The players still had Christmas cake in their feet.
Sergio Cragnotti, *Lazio president, after defeat by Napoli.*

Nicky Laws was flapping about like a kipper out there.

John Barnwell, *Notts County manager*

We held them for 89 minutes and then they kippered us.
Dogon Arif, *Fisher Athletic manager*

You get the ball in the bollocks, in the nose, the gob, and I don't care if it knocks out their ruddy crowns. I've got lads prepared to get it in the kipper. But you don't turn your back and let it hit you in the arse and spin the top corner of the net.
Mick McCarthy, *Wolves manager*

The only problem I have with players today is their music in the dressing room, which is just garbage.
Walter Smith, *Rangers manager*

You hear that rock music and it makes you want to throw yourself off a cliff.

Micah Richards

Andy Cole raps the way he talks and if you've ever heard him talk, you don't want to hear him rap.

Neil McCormick, Daily Telegraph *music critic, reviewing the striker's rap single*

People say footballers have got terrible taste in music but I'd dispute that. In my car at the moment I've got The Corrs, Cher, Phil Collins, Shania Twain and Rod Stewart.

Andy Gray

In Japan there's no decent food, the beer's dead expensive, you can't get drugs, the women are ugly and everyone's too nice. No wonder Gary Lineker went there.

Noel Gallagher of Oasis

13: 'Stabbed in the front': The anatomy of football

We shot ourselves in the foot and I can't stand by and let that happen.
Owen Coyle, *Burnley manager*

We kept kicking ourselves in the foot.
Ray Wilkins

I stuck my foot out and it hit me on the heel, so I'll have to take it on the chin.
Chris Iwelumo, *Scotland striker, after missing an open goal v Norway*

He's gone behind my back right in front of my face.
Craig Bellamy *on Graeme Souness, his manager at Newcastle*

Bobby Gould thinks I'm trying to stab him in the back, but I'm right behind him.
Stuart Pearson, *Gould's assistant at West Brom*

I broke my neck and I haven't looked back since.
Paul Gascoigne

They had more legs than us.
Kenny Sansom *on why Germany beat England in the Legends tournament*

They've kicked our backsides so we've got to lick our wounds.
Steve Bruce *after Wigan's 3-0 defeat to Arsenal*

Last year I had a foot operation. Then my thigh went. This season I'm going to play it by ear.
John Aldridge

It was a head-butt so we'll have to take it on the chin.
Sean O'Driscoll, *Doncaster manager, after Paul Heffernan was sent off*

Tore [Andre Flo] has a groin strain and he's been playing with it.
Alex McLeish *at Rangers*

The Achilles heel that has bitten us in the backside all year stood out like a sore thumb.

Andy King, *Swindon manager*

We were done by our Achilles heel, which has been stabbing us in the back all season.

David O'Leary, *Aston Villa manager*

Our Achilles heel came back to bite us.

Tony Mowbray, *West Brom manager*

My ankle injury has been a real pain in the arse.

David Prutton, *Southampton midfielder*

John Spencer's hamstring is making alarm bells ring in my head.

Craig Brown

Steve McClaren will have a sharp, canny pair of shoulders to listen to.

David Platt

Mick McCarthy keeps his heart on his shirt and his sleeve on his shirt.

Steve Bull

I just wonder what would have happened if the shirt had been on the other foot.
Mike Walker, *Norwich manager*

We've got to roll our sleeves up and get our knees dirty.
Howard Wilkinson *at Sunderland*

Obviously for Scunthorpe it will be a nice scalp to put Wimbledon on their bottoms.

Dave Bassett

Nigeria are going to have to pull their finger out but it is not going to be easy as their backs are against the wall.
John Salako

Mark McGhee is covering his backside in a way that takes the biscuit.
Graham Taylor

We can only come out of this game with egg on our faces, so it's a real banana skin.
Ray Stewart, *Stirling Albion manager*

If they think we'll be easy meat we'll end up with egg on our faces.
Terry Dolan, *Bradford City manager*

It's a case of putting all our eggs into the next 90 minutes.
Phil Neal

I've got irons in the fire and things up my sleeve.
Steve McMahon, *Swindon manager*

I've got other irons in the fire, but I'm keeping them close to my chest.
John Bond *on leaving the Manchester City manager's job*

If you can't stand the heat in the dressing room, get out of the kitchen.
Terry Venables

They've got to stop this runaway train at the top of the Premier League tree and look after the grass roots.
David Pleat

The cat's among the pigeons and meanwhile we're stuck in limbo.
Bernie Slaven, *Middlesbrough striker*

Our back four were at sixes and sevens.
Ron Atkinson *at Aston Villa*

It has left a bad taste in the eyes of our supporters.
Jim Docherty *on problems in the Celtic boardroom*

It's the carrot at the end of the rainbow.
Danny McGrain

I can see the carrot at the end of the tunnel.
Stuart Pearce

If we could bring some silverware to the club that would be a nice little rainbow at the end of a dark tunnel.
Terry McDermott, *Newcastle coach*

Tottenham haven't thrown in the towel even though they've been under the gun.
Bobby Robson

I felt a lump in my throat when the ball went in.
Terry Venables

If they keep ramming it down his throat, the ball's in his court.
Roy Evans, *Liverpool manager*

My heart was in my hands.
Ricky Sbragia

At the end of the day it's not the end of the world.
Jim McLean *at Dundee United*

The tide is very much in our court now.
Kevin Keegan, *Manchester City manager*

No one wants to commit hari-kari and sell themselves down the river.

Gary Lineker *playing for England at Euro 92*

I've sewn a few seeds and thrown a few hand grenades. Now I'm waiting for the dust to settle so I can see how the jigsaw pieces together.
Gary Johnson, *Yeovil manager*

Although we're playing Russian roulette, we're obviously playing Catch 22 at the moment.
Paul Sturrock, *Plymouth manager*

When it becomes a two-horse race it's a different kettle of fish.

Gary Johnson, *Bristol City manager*

There is a rat in the camp trying to throw a spanner in the works.
Chris Cattlin, *Brighton manager*

I had a contract offer on the table but it was swept from under the rug.
Chris Perry *on leaving Charlton*

You can't switch the lights on every time and we didn't smell that one coming. The car was in neutral and we couldn't put it in drive.
Glenn Hoddle *at Tottenham*

No one's shirt is cast in stone.
Glenn Hoddle *as England manager*

I never heard a minute's silence like that.
Glenn Hoddle *at Wembley after Princess Diana's death*

That chance came to him on a plate out of the blue.
Glenn Hoddle

No one hands you cups on a plate.
Terry McDermott, *Newcastle assistant manager*

It was a once-in-a-lifetime experience and hopefully I can repeat it on Saturday.

Alfie Potter, *Kettering Town player*

Our tactics will be all-out attack mixed with caution.
Jimmy McLaughlin, *Shamrock Rovers manager*

The plastic pitch is a red herring.
Graham Taylor *on Oldham's synthetic surface*

What I said to them at half-time would be unprintable on radio.
Gerry Francis, *Tottenham manager*

When their second goal went in, I knew our pig was dead.
Danny Williams, *Swindon manager*

If we played like that every week, we wouldn't be so inconsistent.

Bryan Robson, *Manchester United captain*

Sometimes we're predictable, but of that predictability we're unpredictable.
John Beck, *Cambridge United manager*

We've haven't been good consistently. We're consistent but inconsistent. Inconsistently consistent.

David James, *Manchester City goalkeeper*

If I was still at Ipswich, I wouldn't be where I am today.

Dalian Atkinson, *Aston Villa striker*

In terms of a 15-round boxing match we're not getting past round one. Teams will pinch your dinner from your noses. If you don't heed the warnings, you get nailed to the cross.

Gordon Milne, *Leicester manager*

We're halfway round the Grand National course with many hurdles to clear. So let's all keep our feet firmly on the ground.

Mike Bailey, *Charlton manager*

My team won't freeze in the white-hot atmosphere of Anfield.

Ron Saunders, *Aston Villa manager*

Even when you're dead, you shouldn't let yourself lie down and be buried.

Gordon Lee, *Everton manager*

I'd shoot myself if I had the bottle.

Vinnie Jones *after being sent off for the tenth time*

14: 'Pigs and troughs': The genius of gibberish

I'm not so much disappointed, just disappointed.
***Kevin Keegan**, England manager*

That decision, for me, was almost certainly definitely wrong.
Kevin Keegan

People will say that was typical City, which really annoys me. But that's typical City, I suppose.
***Kevin Keegan** at Manchester City*

We miss Maine Road but we don't really miss it.
Kevin Keegan

The players have got to pick themselves up and we've got to help pick them up.
Kevin Keegan back at Newcastle

They compare Steve McManaman to Steve Heighway. He's nothing like him but I can see why – it's because he's different.
Kevin Keegan

Luis Figo is totally different to David Beckham, and vice versa.
Kevin Keegan

Young Gareth Barry, you know, he's young.
Kevin Keegan

England can end the millennium as it started it, as the greatest football nation in the world.
Kevin Keegan

I'm reluctant to tell you all I know because I really don't know anything.
Kevin Keegan after Newcastle appointed Dennis Wise

Argentina are the second best team in the world and there's no higher praise than that.
Kevin Keegan

Argentina won't be at Euro 2000 because they're from South America.

Kevin Keegan

The 33- and 34-year-olds will be 37 and 38 by the time the next World Cup comes round, if they're not careful.
Kevin Keegan

England have the best fans in the world, and Scotland's are second to none.
Kevin Keegan

I've been interested in racing all my life, or longer really.
Kevin Keegan

We've managed to wrong a few rights.
Kevin Keegan

Coventry equalised with literally the last throw of the dice.
Kevin Keegan after Newcastle were taken to extra time

Goalkeepers aren't really born today until they're in their thirties.
Kevin Keegan

At this level, if five or six players don't turn up you'll get beat.
Kevin Keegan

Football is all about pigs and troughs.
Glenn Hoddle

It's 60-40 against his being fit, but he's got half a chance.
Glenn Hoddle, *Wolves manager*

Five per cent of me is disappointed [to finish second in the group] while the other 50 per cent is just happy that we've qualified.
Michael Owen *with the England squad*

We must have had 99 per cent of the match. It was the other three per cent that cost us.

Ruud Gullit *at Chelsea*

We scored three today and 99 times out of 10 that means a win.
Dean White, *Brighton assistant manager*

I have a feeling everyone is putting two and two together and making four.
Chris Coleman

My parents have always been there for me, ever since I was about seven.
David Beckham

I'm hoping to get back in the team, but they have been doing well, so it's a Catch 23 situation.

Ian Murray, *Rangers player, on returning after injury*

We got a dozen corners, maybe 12, I'm guessing.

Craig Brown

Ninety-nine per cent of two-footed players are right-footed. You don't see many left-footed two-footed players these days.

Joe Royle

There was nothing between us and United, apart from the seven goals.

Danny Wilson *after Barnsley lost 7-0 at Old Trafford*

I don't know whether he wants a No. 2.

Alan Shearer *on Kevin Keegan's possible search for an assistant*

Lightning can strike twice in a one-off cup tie.

Nigel Clough, *Derby manager*

You never know what's going to happen in a couple of one-off games like these.

Graeme Sharp *before two-leg England v Scotland play-off*

Chester made it very difficult for us by getting two men sent off.
John Docherty, *Bradford City manager*

You three are a pair of bastards.
John Lambie, *Partick Thistle manager*

That's understandable, and I understand that.
Terry Venables, *England coach*

There's certainly no uncertainty about my future.
Roy Keane *shortly before resigning as Sunderland manager*

Some of our defending was indefensible.
Mark Hughes, *Manchester City manager*

The new manager has given us unbelievable belief.
Paul Merson *on Arsene Wenger*

He's such an honest person it's untrue.
Brian Little *on Ian Taylor*

The unthinkable is not something we're thinking about.
Peter Kenyon, *chief executive of Manchester United*

People have said it's psychological, but in my head I know that's not true.
Louis Saha *on his injury problems*

This for me is without exception possibly my last World Cup.
Ray Wilkins

I'm not a believer in luck, but I do believe you need it.
Alan Ball, *Manchester City manager*

We can beat anyone on our day, so long as we score.
Alex Totten

It's interesting that the games in which we've dropped points are those where we've failed to score.
Sir Alex Ferguson

You always lose when your opponents score and you don't.

Raymond Domenech

We were in an awkward position against Yugoslavia – in order to win we needed to score more goals than they did.
José Antonio Camacho, *Spain coach*

If corner-kicks hadn't been invented, this would have been a very close game.
Neil Warnock *after Sheffield United lost 4-1 at Newcastle*

We had enough chances to win the game. In fact we did win it.
Alex Smith, *Aberdeen manager*

Winning doesn't really matter as long as you win.

Vinnie Jones

You can't win in football unless you win.
Tony Mowbray *at West Bromwich Albion*

It was a draw so in the end we didn't win.
David Beckham *after Manchester United v Croatia Zagreb*

Hopefully, everything goes right and we both get the result we want.
Dave Jones, *Cardiff City manager, before the FA Cup final against Harry Redknapp's Portsmouth*

You can't say my team aren't winners. They've proved that by finishing fourth, third and second in the past three seasons.
Gerard Houllier, *Liverpool manager*

We're moving up the table, which is hopefully the right direction.
Paul Robinson, *Tottenham goalkeeper*

It's only a must-win game if you need to win it.
Roy Aitken, *Birmingham coach*

I wouldn't be bothered if we lost every game as long as we won the league.
Mark Viduka, *Newcastle striker*

The defeat wasn't as bad as it sounds on paper.
Steve McClaren, *England manager*

A draw like this is the kind of once-in-a-lifetime experience that doesn't come around that often.
Steve McClaren *when his Twente Enschede side were paired with Arsenal*

Wayne Rooney is inexperienced but experienced in what he's been through.
Steve McClaren

Always remember that the goal is at the end of the field, not in the middle.

Sven-Göran Eriksson *to his England squad*

Too many players were trying to create or score a goal.
Gerard Houllier *after Liverpool lost to Watford*

Too often we've been on the losing end of a defeat.
Roy Keane *at Sunderland*

If you gave those free kicks all the time, you would be giving them constantly.
Peter Crouch

We're not here to make up the numbers. We're here to just stay in the league.
Paul Jewell, *Wigan manager*

I can see myself staying at Blackburn for the rest of my career, unless I move to another club.
Benni McCarthy

I got into football to play football.
Luke Moore *on joining West Brom*

I've done everything in my career, but this will be something new and different.

Terry Butcher *on joining the Scotland coaching set-up*

If there were no such thing as football, we'd all be frustrated footballers.
Mike Lyons, *Everton defender*

All derbies are the same, and this will be no exception.
Roy Evans, *Liverpool manager*

The English manager I most admire is Arsene Wenger. Even if he is not English.
Luiz Felipe Scolari

Le Tissier was a super striker of the ball but he never played for a big club. If he had we would be talking about him as a super striker of the ball.
Graeme Souness

There are two ways of getting the ball. One is from your own team-mates, and that's the only way.
Terry Venables

Some of the goals were good, but some of them were sceptical.

Sir Bobby Robson

Don't even think about Manchester United and Stoke City in the same breath.
Tony Pulis, *Stoke manager*

I would think it will be a domino effect – when one goes, one comes in.
Bryan Gunn, *Norwich manager, on imminent changes in his squad*

It's a Dutch invention, but we started it in Scotland.
Andy Roxburgh

For some reason a full ground sounds better than an empty one.
Dominic Matteo

We all know that in football, you stand still if you go backwards.
Peter Reid, *Sunderland manager*

We want to go upwards, not stand still and go backwards.

Chris Robinson, *Hearts chief executive*

The Brazilians were South American, the Ukrainians will be more European.

Phil Neville

They wore their socks off.
Nigel Adkins, *Scunthorpe manager*

My players ran their socks into the ground for Manchester United.
Alex Ferguson

I'm north-east born and bred now.
Len Ashurst, *Liverpool-born former Sunderland defender, professing his love for Wearside*

James Beattie has got a massive head. We've just got to find it.
Glenn Whelan, *Stoke midfielder.*

Rightly or wrongly, we've been wronged.
Chris Coleman, *Fulham manager*

I want to get more players through the door while the window is open.

Mark Hughes, *Manchester City manager*

If you don't believe you can win, there's no point getting out of bed at the end of the day.
Neville Southall, *Everton and Wales goalkeeper*

It just hasn't been our day this week.
Steve Bruce *at Wigan*

At the end of the day it's about what we do on the night.

Bryan Hamilton, *Northern Ireland manager*

That's a milestone lifted from around our necks.
Brian Laws, *Sheffield Wednesday manager*

We're stuck between a rock and the hard stuff.
Mark Wright, *Chester manager*

The gaffer says he's backing me to the hills.
Cameron Jerome, *Birmingham striker*

It leaves a nasty taste in my nostrils.
Jim Magilton, *Ipswich manager, after derby defeat by Norwich*

We didn't get the run of the mill.
Glenn Hoddle, *England manager*

I won't be losing any sleepless nights over it.
Alan Pardew, *West Ham manager*

It has thrown a spanner in the fire.
Bobby Gould, *Wales manager*

It's a war of nutrition.
John Neal, *Middlesbrough manager, on a stand-off with striker Stan Cummins*

I felt as sick as the proverbial donkey.
Mick McCarthy

At the time it happened, I regretted it in hindsight.

Joey Barton

With hindsight, it's easy to look at it with hindsight.
Glenn Hoddle, *England manager*

When you're dealing with someone who has only a pair of underpants on and you take them off, he has nothing left. He is naked. You're better off trying to find him a pair of trousers, to complement him rather than change him.
Arsene Wenger

Maybe we were lucky today, but sometime in the season we will have unluck, as you say.

Sven-Göran Eriksson *after Manchester City beat United*

We need a point as soon as possible, the tooter the sweeter.
Sir Bobby Robson *at Newcastle*

The decisions decided a lot of things, but I'll leave other people to decide.
David O'Leary *bemoans a referee at Aston Villa*

Extra time probably came at the wrong time for us.
Mark Hughes *at Blackburn*

At two down I'd have given my right arm for a draw, but I'm glad I didn't as I wouldn't have been able to clap the fans at the end.
Gary Peters, *Shrewsbury manager*

We weren't beaten today, we lost.

Howard Wilkinson, *Sunderland manager, after his team scored three own goals*

I can't tell you what's going to happen tomorrow, only today. And I can't even tell you what's going to happen today.

David Pleat

The door is always open until it is closed.

Hope Powell, *England women's team manager*

The moral of the story is not to listen to those who tell you not to play the violin but stick to the tambourine.

José Mourinho *at Chelsea*

The ambition of an England manager should be to become England manager.

Graham Taylor, *former England manager*

One accusation you can't throw at me is that I've always done my best.

Alan Shearer

Steve Coppell is out with an inkle anjury.
Jimmy Armfield

Sir Alex is a work alcoholic.
Gerard Houllier, *Liverpool manager*

The status quo remains the same.
Mick McCarthy, *Wolves manager*

What happened? I cannot explanate it.
Emmanuel Adebayor

Sometimes you have to swallow the unswallowable.

Arsene Wenger

I read Michael Caine's biography. It was about him growing up.
Frank Lampard

Our qualifying campaign was a successful failure.

Kenny Miller *on Scotland's bid to reach Euro 2008*

If I have to move on from Newcastle, hopefully it will be to somewhere else.
Joe Kinnear

There are kids out there who'd chop their legs off to play football for Brighton.
Robbie Savage

I'm not superstitious. It brings bad luck.
Raymond Domenech, *France coach*

I don't like going to bed at night with only one left-back.

Peter Taylor, *Wycombe Wanderers manager*

It was good to see them train and get a feel of them.
George Burley, *Scotland manager*

Against Wycombe we ran out winners by one goat to nil.
Dagenham & Redbridge *website*

I like wingers who veer, but I prefer them to veer straight.
Billy Elliott, *Sunderland manager*

Hoddle hasn't been the Hoddle we know, and neither has Robson.

Ron Greenwood, *England manager*

We were up against players who have got names.
Tony Pulis, *Stoke manager, after drawing at Newcastle*

We just have to get our heads down and continue to start winning games.
Carlos Edwards, *Sunderland winger*

It's just a case of crossing the i's and dotting the t's.
Dave Bassett

At the end of today's third round, players you've never heard of will be household names – like that fellow who scored for Sutton United against Coventry last season.
Bobby Campbell, *Chelsea manager*

I definitely want Brooklyn to be christened, though I don't know into which religion.
David Beckham

The Pope was smaller than I expected, but only in size.
Jack Charlton *after visiting the Vatican*

This guy is small but he has the mental strength of a mountain.

Arsene Wenger on Eduardo

I'm sure you'll have a field day in December, come January.

Tony Adams, *Portsmouth manager*

Rome wasn't built in two days.

Danny Bergara, *Rotherham manager*

Africa? We're not in bloody Africa, are we?

Gordon Lee, *Everton manager, when asked his impressions of the continent in Morocco*

Q: Who's going to win Euro 2008?
A: Erm, I've got to go for England... If you can't have faith in your own country, what can you do?
Q: I'm afraid to say we haven't qualified.
A: Oh no, of course. Argentina, then. I'll go for them.

Richard Chaplow, *Preston midfielder, in a programme interview*

I don't like teams that wear stripes. They never win anything.

Derek Dougan *on why he did not want the West Brom manager's job*